The Mindful Way

Mood Swings

Managing anger, anxiety and low mood

CAROLINE MITCHELL

For Dad

First published in Great Britain in 2017

Sheldon Press
36 Causton Street
London SW1P 4ST
www.sheldonpress.co.uk

British Library Cataloguing-in-Publication Data
A catalogue record for this book is available from the British Library

ISBN 978-1-84709-459-9
eBook ISBN 978-1-84709-460-5

Typeset by Fakenham Prepress Solutions, Fakenham, Norfolk NR21 8NN
First printed in Great Britain by Ashford Colour Press
Subsequently digitally printed in Great Britain

eBook by Fakenham Prepress Solutions, Fakenham, Norfolk NR21 8NN

Produced on paper from sustainable forests

Contents

Acknowledgements

First, I am indebted to Fiona Marshall at Sheldon Press for commissioning me to write this book. You have been amazingly supportive and wonderfully patient in answering my many questions, and have given me great guidance throughout! Thank you also to Eilidh McGregor and Rob MacRae for your great advice and support at the start of this process, to Ruth for your frank disclosures regarding your personal experiences with mood swings, and to Carol Walker for all your help and keeping me (relatively) sane. Finally, thanks to family and friends for their kind words of encouragement and accommodating my own individual mood swings during the writing of this book!

Introduction

Have you ever reached over to grab the last piece of chocolate in a bar, only to find out you've already finished it, or gone upstairs to fetch something and forgotten what it was you wanted? My own personal nemesis was arriving at the supermarket minus shopping list (left on the kitchen table), forgetting about a third of what was on the list, then getting home and realizing my credit card was still in the card reader. Any of this sound familiar?

All the above are perfect examples of the kind of mindless behaviour we all exhibit regularly when we're on autopilot and not paying attention to what we're doing. Time and again, we're not truly 'present' in our daily lives as we're so busy with work, family, friends and ever-increasing pressures coming at us from all sides that we don't notice what's going on around us and don't listen when our bodies are telling us to slow down. It's not surprising that so many of us find our moods are unpredictable and seem unmanageable.

Mindfulness teaches us to take time out and understand more about who we are, what's going on in our lives and what we want. Just concentrating on what we think and feel may not initially appear to offer a solution, but if we do this without judging ourselves or others, it's a tremendously empowering experience and one that can change our lives for the better. Mindfulness helps us recognize what the triggers and warning signs are for our mood swings, so we can be more in control of them. Not only can mindfulness work wonders on our mood swings but it can also strengthen our relationships, improve our performance at work and give us a much-needed sense of calm.

Over the last decade or so, the popularity of mindfulness has grown substantially and many high-profile celebrities, including Oprah Winfrey, Davina McCall, Emma Watson and Angelina Jolie, have revealed that they practise it. There's barely a week that passes without a mention of mindfulness in the press. For example, Greater Manchester Police offered some lunchtime mindfulness meditation sessions to its members of staff,[1] to help them counter anxiety and depression and cope with a number of gang-related deaths. The American comedian Ruby Wax,[2] who also holds a Masters degree in mindfulness-based cognitive therapy from Oxford University, has led an all-party mindfulness session for MPs and peers at Westminster to explore a potential role for mindfulness in health, education and criminal justice. Teachers at a primary school in Brighton[3] have started up 15-minute mindfulness sessions for the children to help them learn self-regulation, calm them down and boost their spirits. The evidence base for mindfulness is steadily increasing, too, with many clinical trials already proving its efficacy and indicating that further research is warranted.

Anyone can take up mindfulness at any age. You don't need any qualifications, nor any particular equipment or special clothing to start. You just need somewhere comfortable to sit and a bit of peace and quiet.

This book is a guide to how to handle your mood swings better with mindfulness, and is suitable for people with no prior experience of mindfulness as well as those who have previously 'dabbled'. It takes a look at what mood swings are and how they can affect us, explains what mindfulness is and how it works, discusses how mindfulness can help with mood swings, offers some practical mindfulness exercises for you to follow in relation to your mood swings and, finally, suggests a few simple lifestyle changes that may help. The information given here about mood swings is an overview of what can be a complex mechanism of interacting processes and is not intended to replace medical advice or diagnose any medical or psychological condition, so if you have any concerns, please consult your GP.

1

About mood swings

What are mood swings?

We all have mood swings – they are a natural part of life. At their simplest, mood swings are just a change in how you feel. We have all experienced a shift in our mood from angry to relieved, happy to sad, lively to lethargic. Such shifts can vary in intensity from subtle and barely noticeable to extreme and all-consuming. Mood swings can happen when you're just having a bad day, are nobody's fault and normally subside over time. A certain amount of stress is inevitable and can be a good thing, as it motivates us to get things done and achieve deadlines. More problematic are mood swings that become extreme, change rapidly and start to interfere with your daily functioning, often having an impact on others' lives too.

Who gets mood swings and what causes them?

As we have seen, anyone can get mood swings. They may occur in response to a particular trigger, be caused by a combination of factors or just come out of the blue. Statistics for mood swings are hard to determine, as people tend not to visit their GP specifically to talk about mood swings, but the UK-based mental health charity Mind estimates that 1 in 4 people in the UK experiences a mental health difficulty of some kind each year.[1] By 2030, it is estimated that, in the UK, there will be approximately 2 million more adults with mental health concerns than in 2013, if the prevalence rate of 1 in 4 remains the same.[2]

Several theories have been proposed as to what it is exactly that causes mood swings. Many researchers believe an imbalance in neurotransmitters (chemicals in the brain, such as serotonin, dopamine, noradrenaline and gamma-aminobutyric acid – GABA) cause mood swings, and several brain-imaging studies indicate that the structure and function of the brain differs in people with mood disorders. Many people get low moods as winter approaches, which is likely to be related to the reduction in sunlight, or there may be a genetic tendency towards mood swings. Equally, it might just be that mood swings are part of your personality.

Significant life events

Mood swings are much more common when we experience bereavements, job changes, conflicts, relocation, parenthood, separation or divorce, as it takes time to adjust to a new and sometimes unwanted lifestyle. Longer-term mood swings are likely to occur at times of chronic stress caused by unresolved sexual, emotional or physical traumas.

Lack of sleep

People who do not get enough sleep are generally more irritable and emotionally volatile as a result. Researchers investigating the relationship between insomnia and bipolar disorder have demonstrated that sleep deprivation causes increased activity in the amygdala, which is a key area in the brain responsible for processing emotional reactions, including anxiety and aggression.[3] They have further suggested that the rapid eye movement (REM) phase of sleep, known to be negatively affected by insomnia, is vital for processing emotions.

Food, alcohol and drugs

Surprisingly, some everyday foods can be responsible for mood swings, including highly processed foods, chocolate, cakes, biscuits, crisps and sugar-rich soft drinks. Comfort eating causes a rapid rise in blood sugar levels, providing a quick energy hit, but the subsequent surge in insulin release results in the inevitable slump, low mood and irritability (see page 98), especially after overeating. Caffeine-rich drinks and foods can cause the heart rate to increase, especially after consuming large amounts, often leaving you feeling jittery (see pages 100–1).

Although we generally associate drinking alcohol with being more outgoing, it acts as a depressant in the body, and excessive use can lead to depressive episodes (see pages 101–2). Anyone who has tried to give up smoking will be aware of mood swings, in particular irritability, which is associated with nicotine withdrawal. Illegal drugs (see page 102), such as cocaine and amphetamines, increase the heart rate and can trigger anxiety attacks, with the come-down and associated mood changes lasting perhaps days. Ecstasy can leave you feeling anxious and confused, and some users experience panic attacks. Cannabis, often considered to be a 'milder' drug, may induce anxiety as well as paranoia, and there are conflicting opinions among researchers and health professionals regarding its association with depression.

Age-related mood swings

The likelihood of experiencing mood swings increases during certain phases of our lives, often for physiological reasons. As toddlers reach various developmental milestones, they learn many social, emotional and physical skills all at once, and frustration and tantrums inevitably ensue. Mood swings in school-age children should be investigated, as this may indicate bullying. Exam periods can be particularly troublesome for some youngsters, as can the period leading up to results day.

Puberty brings rapidly surging levels of sex hormones, which play havoc with teenagers' ability to regulate their emotions (as well as with the emotions of their families!). Much research has shown that the teenage brain continues to develop structurally; this is particularly true of the prefrontal cortex, which is responsible for reasoning and impulse control. Understanding that the brain undergoes significant changes over a period of years explains the mood swings, angry outbursts and apparently irrational behaviour of many teenagers. Pregnancy is renowned for mood swings, as are the perimenopausal and menopause periods, as hormone levels fluctuate dramatically. Particularly susceptible to low moods, elderly people often withdraw socially and, as many believe that mental health issues carry a stigma, they are likely to hide how they feel.

Medical conditions

Mood swings may be symptomatic of a medical concern, but it does not mean you have a medical disorder if you get mood swings. It is vital not to self-diagnose or self-medicate if you believe a medical condition is causing your mood swings – you must get a proper diagnosis from a medical professional, who will help you to access the enormous amount of support available. Many people view being given a diagnosis of, for example, bipolar

disorder as a relief rather than a negative label: it is con-
firmation that they are not losing their mind or having a
nervous breakdown.

Intense and uncontrollable mood swings are more likely
to indicate an underlying medical concern. Bipolar disorder, previously known as manic depression, is probably
the most well-known mood disorder and is characterized
by severe episodes of mania and low mood lasting weeks
or longer. Often starting with sleeplessness, irritability
and loss of appetite, the mania phase carries a certain
appeal in that increased levels of creativity and capability
are experienced, so you feel like you have huge amounts
of energy and could conquer the world. Mania, however,
encourages risky and impulsive behaviours and may
be associated with delusions, hallucinations and even
psychosis.

The depressive phase may begin with a sensation of
something switching off in the brain, almost as if you
know what's coming. During this phase, you are likely
to become withdrawn and uninterested, feel worthless,
hopeless and lethargic, lack confidence, have suicidal
thoughts and dread getting up in the morning – everything seems much more of a big deal than previously.

Bipolar disorder is relatively common and does not
appear to be more prevalent in either sex. The NHS estimates that 1 in every 100 adults will be diagnosed with
bipolar disorder, although it is uncommon to develop

it after the age of 40.[4] Celebrities have brought much-needed publicity to and more understanding of this condition in more recent years. Stephen Fry's courageous battle with the condition, for example, hit the headlines and was featured in the 2006 BBC documentary *The Secret Life of the Manic Depressive*.[5]

Extreme mood swings are common in borderline personality disorder (otherwise known as emotionally unstable personality disorder), in which people also exhibit impulsive behaviours, have abandonment issues, tend to form unstable relationships, struggle to control anger, can self-harm and may experience suicidal thoughts and paranoia. The UK-based charity Rethink Mental Illness estimates that 1 in 100 people has borderline personality disorder.[6]

In addition to chronic low mood, depressive disorders may involve changeable moods, including agitation and anger. The fifth edition of the *Diagnostic and Statistical Manual of Mental Disorders* (DSM-5),[7] the leading authority on psychiatric diagnoses, lists further medical conditions in which mood swings are a key symptom, such as cyclothymia (a milder form of bipolar disorder), dysthymia and anxiety disorders. Damage to the frontal lobe of the brain, which helps control emotions, can occur following a stroke or traumatic brain injury or with certain kinds of dementia, and may lead to angry outbursts. Fluctuations in mood can also be caused by low blood sugar, thyroid imbalance, anaemia, seasonal affective disorder, postnatal depression, multiple sclerosis, meningitis, brain tumours, conditions where the brain has been deprived of nutrients or oxygen and some cardiovascular and digestive tract diseases. In children, mood swings are a key symptom of attention deficit hyperactivity disorder (which also occurs in adults) and oppositional defiant disorder.

What happens to the body during mood swings?

People who experience mood swings are only too aware of the emotional impact and long-term effects – frequent headaches, recurring aches and pains, difficulties concentrating, feeling lethargic, too much or too little sleep, excessive sweating and reduced libido are all common. Mood swings cause many different physical responses too, as briefly discussed below.

In the brain

Many of the physiological effects of anger and anxiety are similar. When we feel very anxious, the part of the brain responsible for survival instincts, the limbic system (specifically, the amygdala), recognizes a potential threat and the body's fight–flight–freeze reaction is initiated. In a highly complex cascade of reactions, various hormones and neurotransmitters (for example, catecholamines such as adrenaline, noradrenaline and dopamine) are released, which ultimately raise blood pressure, increase blood sugar levels and provide a surge of energy – responses designed to prime your body to confront the threat (fight), run away from it (flight) or dissociate from it (freeze). Also released by the brain are endorphins, the body's natural painkillers, which reduce the impact of any pain you may experience.

All these physical reactions occur within a few seconds of perceiving a threat and we have very little control over them. This incredible energy rush is responsible for the impulsive feeling that makes an angry person's reactions unpredictable. After this initial surge of activity, certain areas in the brain, which modulate our reasoning, then evaluate the threat and allow us to moderate our actions. These responses can be life-saving when the threat is real; however, with extreme mood swings, the body is constantly on alert. Being in this state for short or longer periods can leave you feeling exhausted and prone to low mood.

Low mood itself can be associated with reduced levels of the neurotransmitters that regulate pain perception, meaning you are more susceptible to feeling pain sensations, particularly in the back. Chronic low mood is thought to be connected with a lack of concentration and poor memory. A study carried out in 2014 showed that people with chronic stress can develop long-term alterations in the brain rendering them more susceptible to extreme anxiety and mood disorders.[8]

In the circulatory system

Stress and anger induce the release of hormones such as adrenaline, cortisol and adrenocorticotrophic hormone, leading to an increase in the heart rate and blood pressure; these may cause physiological effects such as your face flushing, a tingling or twitching sensation in your muscles or chest palpitations. In long-term regular mood swings, these hormones are present for protracted periods of time, giving a higher risk of heart disease, blood clots and stroke (the increased risk of a heart attack in the 2 hours following an angry outburst is well documented and long-term low mood is thought to be associated with an increased risk of heart disease). The higher cortisol levels cause the immune system to function less effectively, explaining why people who are chronically stressed or angry are frequently ill.

Some men find that mood swings can cause loss of or difficulty with erections. Levels of oestrogen and progesterone can fluctuate dramatically in women experiencing premenstrual syndrome, causing imbalanced moods. One effect of oestrogen is to stop cells adhering to the inside of blood vessel walls, therefore helping to prevent blockages. As post-menopausal women have reduced levels of oestrogen, they may consequently be more susceptible to heart disease than premenopausal women when exposed to significant anxiety.

In the digestive system

Anxiety is known to exacerbate irritable bowel syndrome (IBS) and stomach upsets by increasing cramping of the muscles in the gut, and longer-term stress is a potential causative factor of stomach ulcers and even intestinal cancers. Extreme stress can cause vomiting and/or the bladder and anal sphincters to relax, clearly not desirable, and some people believe that longer-term anger may be responsible for constipation. Stress and low mood can both cause reduced appetite or overeating, leading to weight gain or loss.

How we regulate our emotions

As children, we learn to deal with emotions by observing how others manage theirs and from the responses we receive when we're upset. We grow up better equipped to handle normal mood fluctuations if we have felt listened to and understood and have been encouraged to appropriately express how we feel from an early age. If, however, we've received largely negative or conflicting messages, we are likely to reach adulthood confused about how to handle emotionally charged situations. We will struggle to express ourselves calmly, become overwhelmed and consequently be more susceptible to mood swings.

Thought processes

The way you think has a direct impact on your emotions. It's not necessarily the situation itself that causes you to feel angry, anxious or down, it's the interpretation and meaning you place on that situation (see page 48). In the 1950s, American psychologist Albert Ellis proposed that what troubles us is governed by basic irrational assumptions, and how we think (our self-talk) and behave reinforces our distress. Our interpretation may not be wholly accurate and tends to carry a negative bias, leading to anger, anxiety and/or low mood. It's important to remember that thoughts are just that – thoughts. They are not facts. In reality, thought processes that support anger, anxiety and low mood can be highly complex. The following is just a brief explanation of what might be behind them.

Anger

A sense of injustice is involved somewhere. Our sense of self-worth has been challenged and we feel vulnerable or believe someone has hurt us. We have been badly treated, we believe we have been attacked in some way or we can't tolerate frustration. Repeatedly reminding ourselves of previous bad experiences, comparing ourselves with others, feeling ignored or rejected – all these fuel anger. Anger as an emotion is not bad in itself as it warns us something isn't right, but it can be very destructive and it is how we handle it that matters. It can also exacerbate anxiety symptoms and has been linked to depression.

Anxiety

Persistent negative thoughts, often involving 'What if . . . ?' scenarios, support anxiety. We spend hours, days or more worrying over something that may not have happened yet. We make assumptions that the future will be terrible and we will have no control over it. Where, though, is the proof that the worst will happen and we will not be able to handle it?

Low mood

During the 1960s and 1970s, American psychiatrist Aaron T. Beck considered how people with low mood experience cycles of negative automatic thoughts that appear to come from nowhere. These thoughts may be about yourself, the world in general or the future and have a common theme of a persistently negative outlook. Ruminating, repeatedly focusing on negative aspects of the past, will make your low mood worse. Low mood may also be associated with the loss of something (for example, redundancy or a death) or the lack of something you want – all underpinned by negative thoughts.

It is highly likely that specific thoughts are behind your mood swings. Mindfulness addresses how you think, as do cognitive behavioural therapy (CBT) and other therapies and strategies (see Chapter 3).

When you should seek help

Mood swings are normal reactions to life's events and usually subside over time, but when they are frequent and intense with no apparent triggers, don't go away over time or form a rapidly changing cyclical pattern, it might be time to ask for help.

Below is a list of thoughts, emotions and behaviours – if these warning signs feature significantly in your life, it may indicate your mood swings are out of control or perhaps be symptomatic of bipolar disorder or another medical condition.

- **Increased risk-taking behaviour** This includes sexual promiscuity, not taking appropriate safe sex precautions (with the resultant potential of contracting a sexually transmitted disease and/or having an unwanted pregnancy), driving irresponsibly (which has legal consequences), gambling more than you can afford to lose and excessive spending habits (leading to financial problems).
- **Delusions of grandeur** An intense feeling of invincibility and the conviction that you can conquer the world, even believing you may be 'Jesus Christ reborn'.
- **Instantly empathizing with what you see on the TV or read in magazines** Feeling convinced that many things are directly and intentionally related to you.

- **A sense of paranoia** Everything feels like it's your fault, even things that don't directly involve you.
- **Self-harm** Includes cutting or burning, picking your skin until it bleeds, pulling your hair out, binge eating or neglecting your well-being in other ways that help you cope.
- **Suicidal thoughts** Encompasses a wide spectrum of intent – fleeting thoughts, researching suicide on the internet or planning how/when to do it. Passing thoughts of suicide during times of crisis are normal, but dwelling on it or feeling calmer when you have made plans is a very strong warning sign.
- **Drug or alcohol use and substance abuse** Moderate alcohol consumption or the occasional use of recreational drugs is a generally fairly harmless way to unwind. When their use becomes your primary coping mechanism, however, ironically it worsens your mood swings and the additional threat of addiction exists.
- **Struggling to control anger** Anger is not just shouting – it manifests as irritability, passive aggression (such as intentionally annoying others), threatening behaviour, violence or needing to walk away from people if you are concerned that you may get violent.
- **Relationship difficulties** Constantly arguing with everyone or others saying you are difficult to be around because of your moodiness and unpredictability.

- **Preoccupation with past traumatic experiences** Previous incidents such as abuse, assaults or accidents that 'haunt' you and seem current, even months or years later.
- **Frequent thoughts of having low self-worth** Intense, pervasive and almost paralysing negative thoughts about yourself, such as you'll never find a job, be successful or have a good relationship because you don't deserve it.
- **Numbness when highly stressed** Feeling distant is normal – zoning out when you're bored, for example – but dissociation as a routine response is not ideal.
- **Deliberately breaking the law** Having a 'catch me if you can' attitude. It's only a matter of time before something will catch up with you, at which point damage to yourself or others could be irreparable and you may face criminal charges.

How many of the above can you tick off as experiencing regularly or to extremes? It is important to emphasize that identifying with a few of these points in the short term is normal, but if most of them are familiar to you, it's time to seek advice.

Your first step has been to recognize that you are struggling; the next step is to take action.

Where to go for help

If you identify significantly with many points on the list, your first stop should be your GP (if you are not currently registered with a doctor, it's easy to get one – see 'NHS', Useful resources, page 113). Your doctor will ask questions about what you are experiencing and what effect it is having on your life, and may use some questionnaires to clarify the intensity of your mood swings. You may be referred to a psychiatrist for a specific diagnosis or have a blood test to rule out a medical condition. It is important to have as much information as possible so you fully understand what is happening to you.

Uncertainty about seeing a doctor concerning 'mental health' concerns is very common. An article released on the NHS England website in October 2013 reported that over a third of GP appointments relate to mental health issues, amounting to about 150 million consultations each year.[9] Every 7 years, a household survey is carried out in England to determine what these issues are.[1] The 2009 report found that, for every 100 people, 2.6 experience depression, 4.7 have anxiety and 9.7 people report mixed anxiety and depression each year (that's a total of 17 per cent of people). In 2013/14, there were almost 3 million adults on local GP registers diagnosed with depression.[10]

From this, it's abundantly clear that you are not alone! If you don't think your usual doctor will understand, however, ask to see another GP at that practice or change surgeries – you're well within your rights to do so. Alternatively, you could find a local counsellor yourself without seeing your GP (see Useful resources, pages 113 and 114). Remember, the more significant your mood swings are, the more severe the impact of them will be on you and, inevitably, on others – therefore the more quickly you get professional support, the better.

Current therapies for mood swings

Many kinds of help are available for mental health concerns, including mood swings. Where a co-morbidity exists (that is, another difficulty in addition to mood swings), such as a reliance on alcohol, it is important to treat that first before addressing your mood swings. Your GP will be able to help decide what form of help is best for you, whether it be counselling, medication or other therapies. The following is a brief overview of the kinds of help available.

Counselling

The stigma associated with counselling and psychotherapy has fortunately become less pronounced in recent years, largely thanks to media campaigns and public disclosures by many celebrities, such as Stephen Fry regarding his struggle with bipolar disorder, footballer David Beckham's history of obsessive-compulsive disorder and singer Lady

Gaga's lifelong battle with anxiety and depression. All forms of counselling help you learn more about your mood swings and their causes, which can be invaluable.

Cognitive behavioural therapy

Cognitive behavioural therapy (CBT) is most commonly used to treat anxiety and depression, and can be effective for bipolar disorder, phobias, eating disorders, anger, substance misuse and relationship difficulties. Based on the concept that your thoughts, emotions, behaviours and physical reactions are interconnected, CBT challenges your specific negative thoughts, checks their accuracy and seeks to change any distorted or extreme views you have of a situation to a more balanced viewpoint. This allows you to break out of a learned cycle of negative thinking and helps stabilize your moods, giving you more control. There is an enormous amount of information about CBT that is readily available.

Other talking therapies

Person-centred counselling is a humanistic approach to psychotherapy involving looking at how you see yourself to identify what prevents you from reaching your full potential. During the sessions, you work very closely with a genuine and non-judgemental therapist to create a relationship whereby you feel unconditionally accepted and able to explore fully deep emotions and difficulties you have experienced. Some people with mood swings find family therapy, involving working with other members of your family, useful, and art therapy can help you to express how you feel.

Therapies developed to treat borderline personality disorder include dialectic behaviour therapy (DBT) and mentalization-based therapy (MBT). DBT investigates triggers that lie behind your mood swings, works to improve your responses and regulates your thoughts. It also involves a mindfulness component that teaches awareness, acceptance and tolerance of your difficulties. MBT investigates your thought processes, helps you to determine how realistic they are and teaches you how to understand the ways in which your behaviour affects others emotionally.

Medication

Prescription medication should only be taken following a formal diagnosis. Many people are reluctant to go down this route, having heard accounts of debilitating side effects and addiction. All medication (including paracetamol) has the potential for side effects, but these are often short term and your GP or pharmacist will be able to offer you advice about managing them while you find the right drug and the optimum dose for you. It is sometimes a case of weighing up the benefits of a more stable mood versus some inconvenient side effects. Prescription medication can, however, work quickly to stabilize your mood and prevent relapses, allowing you to start practising mindfulness so you can learn to manage your mood swings better in the longer term.

Depending on your diagnosis, you may be prescribed the mood stabilizer lithium, an anticonvulsant such as valproate, carbamazepine or lamotrigine (originally designed to treat epilepsy), quetiapine (an antipsychotic), benzodiazepines (for short-term use only) or an anti-depressant, although recent research has questioned the efficacy of antidepressants for mood swings. No drugs are available that specifically target anger. If you have abnormal thyroid hormone levels or high calcium levels, you may be prescribed medication to return these to within normal ranges. Once you start taking any medica-tion, do not stop it suddenly, even if you feel OK – you should reduce the dosage gradually under close medical supervision.

Natural remedies

There are many relaxation techniques that can effect-ively reduce stress, help with low mood and generally have calming effects. These range from simple breathing and counting techniques to more complex visualization methods. Acupuncture is an ancient form of alternative therapy derived from Chinese medicine, in which very fine needles are inserted into specific parts of the body to stimulate the central nervous system. It can be effective in treating some kinds of pain, but its use is not widely valid-ated by clinical trials. One randomized controlled study carried out at Stanford University, California, investigated acupuncture for treating depression during pregnancy in 150 women.[11] The researchers concluded that a short acupuncture protocol reduced symptoms similarly to standard depression treatments and could therefore be a viable treatment option. Acupuncture has the benefit of being entirely natural, so may suit people who prefer not to take medication.

Light therapy

Light, whether from the sun or an artificial light box, is known to improve our mood in general, and alternating light and dark periods are essential for setting our body clocks. There is some evidence to show that people with mood swings are particularly sensitive to light and dark variations. A 2005 study in Italy found that a regime of 14 hours' enforced darkness for three consecutive nights reduced mania scores in bipolar inpatients when they were treated within 2 weeks of the onset of the current manic episode, even allowing some participants to reduce their medication.[12] There has been much speculation among scientists as to how the emission of blue light from TVs, mobile phones and computer screens disturbs our sleep by suppressing the production of melatonin, the sleep hormone. Some authorities recommend a total avoidance of blue light for several hours before bedtime, and using a blue light filter on your devices or glasses can help with this.

2

About mindfulness

Mindless behaviour is something we all exhibit from time to time. Switching on the weather forecast, for example, then zoning out and realizing after it's finished that we've thought of something else the whole way through and have no idea whether there's snow or a heatwave due at the weekend. Another is sitting in a meeting, the speaker is closing the proceedings and we haven't a clue what actions we've agreed to!

Most of us rush through life at 100 miles an hour, trying to do many things at the same time without stopping to consider what's going on for us. While we're doing this, we lose sight of what's happening, don't notice the warning signs, often push ourselves to the limit and generally are unaware of what we're doing to ourselves. Mindfulness is pretty much the polar opposite: it involves being acutely aware of what's happening for ourselves right now.

The National Institute for Health and Care Excellence (NICE),[1] part of the Department of Health, offers guidance and advice for improving health and social care in the UK. In terms of mental health therapies, its guidance is followed by GPs and other health professionals when deciding what treatments are suitable for particular conditions. The past few years have seen mindfulness included in the guidelines for an increasing number of medical and psychological conditions, and the evidence base for its efficacy continues to grow rapidly.

What is mindfulness?

Mindfulness is not a traditional kind of psychotherapy or mode of counselling. It is a deep awareness that we get by really paying attention to the thoughts, emotions and physical sensations we experience and by accepting them in a non-judgemental way. The mind–body understanding we achieve focuses only on what is happening at that precise moment – it is not concerned with what has happened in the past or what may happen in the future. We experience our emotions, even the unpleasant ones, without fighting against them. Mindfulness teaches us to re-evaluate our automatic reactions and consequently respond more calmly to the pressures and demands of everyday life as we become more attuned to what the body is saying. It's about training our minds over time, not merely thinking more positively. The principles of mindfulness have been around for thousands of years and are primarily drawn from Buddhism, particularly the aspects of mindfulness that teach mind–body awareness and encourage compassion and acceptance of suffering (which is usually temporary). Mindfulness is not a religious approach to well-being, however, and can be practised by anyone of any faith as well as by people who have no particular faith. It enables us to take control of our experiences and realize that we have the power to initiate change for ourselves.

Jon Kabat-Zinn, who devised mindfulness, explained it as follows:

> Mindfulness means paying attention in a particular way: on purpose, in the present moment, and nonjudgementally.[2]

This may sound straightforward, but is far from easy!

A brief history of mindfulness

In the late 1970s, Kabat-Zinn, Professor of Medicine Emeritus at the University of Massachusetts Medical School in the USA, developed an 8-week course in mindfulness for people with long-term conditions such as pain and stress. He had previously studied molecular biology at Massachusetts Institute of Technology, and went on to integrate meditation and yoga studies with science to give us mindfulness. This 8-week programme is now known as mindfulness-based stress reduction (MBSR).

In the 1990s, Mark Williams, John Teasdale and Zindel Segal formulated a mindfulness-based cognitive therapy

(MBCT) programme from MBSR, specifically targeting the treatment of recurrent depression. Advances in research over the last few decades have seen the use of MBSR and MBCT expand rapidly, and mindfulness is now practised and taught worldwide to great effect in a variety of situations for a wide range of purposes.

The core concepts of mindfulness

Mindfulness comprises three main components: awareness, being fully present in the here and now, and a non-judgemental attitude. The acknowledgement and acceptance of adversity and suffering is a further key element.

Awareness

Our minds naturally wander, and we can zone out in certain situations. For example, while driving on the motorway, we may momentarily be unaware of what's going on around us. It is normal for our minds to flit from one subject to another, particularly as most of us have very busy lives and we seem to operate on autopilot much of the time.

As Kabat-Zinn has said:

> Meditation is the process by which we go about deepening our attention and awareness, refining them, and putting them to greater practical use in our lives.[2]

In mindfulness, we are not on autopilot: awareness means concentrating on and being attentive to what we are feeling, doing and thinking – seeing things for how and what they really are without attaching any interpretation or judgement and without dwelling on anything. We can be distracted by thoughts, emotions, body sensations, smells and sounds during mindfulness practice – it's OK for this to happen. Just notice what has distracted us, learn to not become absorbed in it, let it go and rein the focus of attention back in. Observing what is happening gives us an outsider's perspective, similar to getting feedback from someone else. This is often an uncomfortable, but usually invaluable, process. Awareness is often considered to be the most important part of mindfulness.

Being fully present in the here and now

Thoughts come and go continually about past events, things that are current for us and situations that might occur in the future. We frequently ruminate about the past – repeatedly focusing on negative events, going over and over things in an attempt to understand what really happened or where we went wrong. The more we focus on negatives from the past and label our thoughts as problems, the more we intensify and prolong our low mood. We recall other bad situations, dwell on those too, sink deeper into a cycle of negative beliefs and lose sight of what our actual reality is at that moment. Many of us also worry, often to excess, about future situations that might not go in our favour or over which we have no control. Our thoughts run wild and we imagine all sorts of terrible scenarios, but this dramatic internal monologue only winds us up and prevents us from fully experiencing the here and now.

It is our thoughts that cause us to feel anxious or down and if these thoughts are not present, we do not experience the negative emotions. By focusing our attention only on what is happening at that moment without creating a new meaning, we are letting go of unhelpful and time-wasting distractions that maybe do not reflect reality or we cannot do anything about. Mindfulness teaches us a decentring process whereby we learn to step back from our thoughts and just observe them, so we do not become our experiences or allow ourselves to be defined by them. After all, we cannot change the past or be certain about exactly how things might pan out in the future. We can only truly influence what's happening right now.

Non-judgemental attitude

We all judge ourselves and other people every day. We learn to do this in childhood from watching how other people interact and react, and by noticing the comments others make. As we grow up, we form belief systems about ourselves and others, how the world functions and what's right and wrong, and we develop a sense of who we are. Our belief systems are often heavily influenced by what our parents, grandparents or other significant people say. We sometimes adopt others' beliefs without questioning their validity. For example, the phrase 'there's no smoke without fire' implies that if negative things are said, there is usually some element of truth in it. We hear about an event in the news, make assumptions and pass judgement without knowing the true facts and the whole picture. In reality, very few things are black and white; life is full of grey areas.

Our sense of self evolves over our lifespan from a combination of our experiences and interpretations. We like to be right and do not like acknowledging that we are wrong, but the reality is that we all have weaknesses, and usually plenty of them! Mindfulness directly encourages us to seek out the truth, which involves acknowledging that we are imperfect. The more we practise mindfulness, the less important it becomes for us to be right; we learn to tolerate our imperfections and accept that we don't have to control everything.

Being present in the here and now in mindfulness terms is not easy. We can become frustrated and believe we cannot do it, pass judgement on our apparent lack of progress and conclude that we are useless at this technique. Instead, a non-judgemental attitude encourages us to accept how, at that moment, we are distracted by a thought, a particular sensation in the body or the sound of someone shouting outside – and that's OK. Distraction is part of the mindfulness learning process, so there's no need to beat ourselves up about it. Once we acknowledge this is what's happening right now without judging, we just refocus our attention and proceed.

Letting go of judgement of ourselves and others is very freeing and empowering, and creates a sense of inner peace. When our attention is diverted during practice, mindfulness encourages us to return our focus with kindness towards ourselves in a gentle and understanding way. A newly developed non-judgemental attitude towards ourselves enables us to feel self-compassion. When this happens, we become more understanding of others' problems too and feel more compassionate towards them. Mindfulness is about striving to accept things as they are, including the bad things, without judging whether they are right or wrong, and this opens us up to other possibilities.

Adversity: accepting life can be a struggle and change is inevitable

In mindfulness, we accept how things are at any given moment and that it's OK to be in that place at that time. We are encouraged to stay with whatever unpleasant emotions we feel and wait for them to subside instead of pushing them away. Being aware of the negatives will feel uncomfortable for a while, but the process of mindfulness teaches us that we are more than just our thoughts and emotions (see page 48) and, by allowing ourselves to experience this process, we consequently suffer less.

This can seem counterintuitive, and you might question the rationale of how focusing on what upsets you can make you less upset, but change is inevitable and so is the sense of uneasiness that usually accompanies it, albeit temporarily.

Teasdale and Chaskalson propose that craving lies at the heart of why we suffer, and our mental processes maintain and reinforce our distress.[3] If there is to be change, at least one of the three strategies listed below is required.

1 We can change the content of our thoughts by intentionally redirecting our focus of attention to something that does not support our suffering (such as a sensation in the body), so we change what the mind is processing (the most straightforward strategy).

2 We can change how we process information by, for example, paying attention to unpleasant feelings but approaching them with an attitude of curiosity and intrigue, perhaps, as opposed to an attitude of aversion and becoming lost in them.

3 We can alter our view of what we are processing and gain a different insight, so instead of taking a situation personally, we can view it as just some unpleasant emotions, thoughts or sensations in the body that we are experiencing at that time.

In mindfulness, we aim to understand what is happening within ourselves without reacting to it. We accept that it is not possible to resolve some things and, although we may have been wronged, we can let it go. The more attention we pay to all things negative, the more we will notice negative things around us. The opposite is also true: when we intentionally focus on the positive aspects of life, we will continue to notice other things of a more positive nature. So when we accept that our suffering is transient and bearable, we open ourselves up to the possibility of change, allowing us to choose what to focus on and how to live, and giving us opportunities for growth, learning and adventure. None of us can avoid suffering, pain and change – they are inevitable parts of life.

What is mindfulness used for?

Mindfulness gives us more than simply a way of feeling better within ourselves. Numerous studies carried out to date strongly support its efficacy for treating medical conditions, and it is included within several psychotherapeutic interventions: MBSR was initially developed to treat stress and pain and was adapted and developed into MBCT, which is a recommended treatment for recurrent depression.

Medical applications

The following is a non-exhaustive list of conditions that may benefit from mindfulness. Please note, however, it is not intended to imply that mindfulness will cure these conditions, but several studies suggest it offers some potential for improvement in many areas, including the following:

- anxiety, stress and panic attacks – regularly practised, mindfulness reduces mental triggers, so anxiety-based attacks are less frequent and less intense, and long-lasting physiological and psychological improvements in certain kinds of anxiety are possible;
- obsessive-compulsive disorder;
- depression, including unipolar and recurrent forms;
- addictions – mindfulness helps to give back a feeling of control back over compulsions to take or do something, such as drugs, smoking, alcohol, exercise, gambling or shopping;
- bipolar disorder and borderline personality disorder;
- immune system disorders;
- pain, especially chronic pain;
- fatigue related to multiple sclerosis;[1]
- complications resulting from brain injuries;
- IBS – as of 2015, mindfulness was listed by NICE as an additional recommendation for IBS;[1]
- improved well-being in cancer patients;
- cardiovascular benefits – mindfulness has been shown to reduce blood pressure and so helps to protect against developing hypertension and reduces the risk and severity of cardiovascular disease; NICE recommends

that mindfulness therapies be considered in self-management plans for people with stable angina;[1]

- psoriasis, as the condition is thought to be exacerbated by stress, which mindfulness helps to reduce;
- eating disorders;
- tinnitus;
- asthma.

Other uses and benefits

Wherever greater emotional regulation is required, mindfulness can help. Even if we do not have anything 'wrong' with us as such, we can all benefit from taking time out each day just for ourselves – if for nothing more than to keep ourselves grounded! When mindfulness becomes part of our lives, it opens up possibilities for our future, as we become less controlled and restricted by our fears. We can use mindfulness in or apply it to most situations, the following being just a few examples.

- **Relationships and interpersonal skills** Mindfulness can drastically improve how we relate to others and communicate, as we learn to become more aware of our own reactions and more supportive and less critical of ourselves and others. We also become more attuned to others, allowing us to focus more intently on conversations rather than being distracted by random thoughts of what is happening later or a meeting at work tomorrow.

- **Self-confidence** When we stop judging, we become less defensive and have less to fear from reprisals by others.
- **Decision-making and problem-solving** Mindfulness can make things seem clearer and simpler, enabling us to be more objective and more measured in our responses.
- **Performance at work** Many people find that mindfulness sharpens their minds and their reactions are calmer; they become more productive and gain a healthier work–life balance. It can also improve your leadership abilities.
- **Memory and learning** In making us think more clearly, mindfulness often helps us to pick up new concepts more easily and we can become more creative.
- In **coaching techniques** and helping us to **reach our potential**.

Can anyone do mindfulness?

Yes, anyone can practise and benefit from mindfulness. Structured programmes are now undertaken worldwide in some hospitals, schools, universities and prisons, in athletics training programmes, in businesses for reducing workplace stress and for team-building purposes.

Specific organizations that have publicly declared the in-house use of mindfulness to improve their employees' well-being include Google, Facebook, the investment bank Goldman Sachs, Transport for London and the Home Office.

Whether you're female or male, young or old, in good or poor health, working or unemployed – mindfulness can be for you. The only prerequisite is a willingness to commit to keep practising, particularly when aspects of it do not come easily. You need to persevere – remember, Rome wasn't built in a day! As with learning anything new, the more we work at it, the easier it gets. There's a physiological basis behind this: Canadian psychologist Donald Hebb, a world leader in neuropsychology, explained in Hebb's Law how the learning process and formation of a habit works:

Neurons that fire together, wire together.[4]

Neurons are cells in the brain that are involved in processing and transmitting electrical and chemical signals. When they are repeatedly stimulated during actions we do over and over again, they form stronger links and function together, which increases efficiency and makes transmission of an impulse easier. So the more we do something, the easier it gets – remember how learning to drive became second nature after a while? The same principle applies with mindfulness practice – if you don't get the hang of it at first, the more you practise, the better at it you will become.

How does mindfulness work?

The evidence base for mindfulness continues to grow, but there is no one definitive theoretical framework that is widely accepted to explain specifically how it works. Mindfulness can help to reduce stress levels, so some researchers have investigated the effect of mindfulness on levels of stress hormones, using cortisol as a biomarker. Some studies show a statistically significant reduction in cortisol levels following mindfulness practice, whereas other studies have not been able to find a significant reduction. It is clear that attention pays a pivotal role in mindfulness meditation, and different researchers propose that the effects of mindfulness come about as the result of several components. The following are just a handful of proposals that can be found in the literature.

In 2004, Bishop et al. put forward a two-component model of mindfulness in which attention is regulated to focus on the immediate current experience, and explained how this experience should be entered into with an attitude of 'curiosity, openness and acceptance'.[5] Three critical components of mindfulness (attention, intention and attitude) were proposed by Shapiro, Carlson, Astin and Freedman (2006),[6] and in 2007 Brown, Ryan and Creswell[7] suggested mechanisms of insight, exposure, non-attachment, enhanced mind–body functioning and integrated functioning. Exposure, cognitive change, self-management, relaxation and acceptance were five components proposed by Baer[8] in a review that may explain how mindfulness works. Hölzel et al.[9] proposed four interacting mechanisms: attention regulation, body awareness, emotional regulation (involving reappraisal, and exposure, extinction and reconsolidation) and a change in perspective on the self. Similarities and different biases exist among the theories proposed to date, and it is clear that mindfulness works via an array of inter-reacting mechanisms.

Demonstrating the effects mindfulness has on the brain

Neuroimaging techniques have demonstrated how mindfulness is associated with neuroplastic changes (the creation of new neural connections that promote efficiency and resilience) in certain regions of the brain, including regions that play a role in emotional processing and facilitating cognitive control. In particular, changes in neurological structure and function have been shown in the anterior cingulate cortex, insula, temporo-parietal junction, frontolimbic network and default mode network structures.[9] Neuroimaging techniques use magnetic or electric fields, radio waves, paramagnetic fields or radioactive tracers to visualize activity in specific parts of the brain and are carried out under strictly controlled conditions. Some well-known imaging techniques include X-rays, magnetic resonance imaging (MRI), computed tomography (CT, also known as computerized axial tomography or CAT) and positron emission tomography (PET).

The following is a very small selection of studies showing some of the differences found in various regions of the brain in people who practise mindfulness regularly compared with those who do not. The full text of these articles is highly complex, often with multiple points being investigated in each study. The summaries listed below are therefore necessarily very brief snapshots of just some of this research.

- Using functional MRI (fMRI) techniques, Hölzel et al.[10] demonstrated that focused attention meditation caused stronger activation in the rostral anterior cingulate cortex region of the brain, suggesting that meditators are more engaged in emotional processing.
- Farb et al.[11] investigated the brain activity that occurred with experiential or narrative focusing in individuals who had undergone MBSR training compared with non-trained control participants. Experiential focusing involved just being aware of thoughts, feelings and physical reactions from one moment to the next and returning to the current experience whenever distracted, whereas during narrative focusing individuals were asked to judge what was happening and evaluate what it meant to them. fMRI studies showed that individuals who had had the mindfulness training showed

larger reductions in activity in the medial prefrontal cortex during experiential compared with narrative focusing. Other differences in brain activity were also seen in the two types of focusing, as well as between the trained and non-trained participants.

- Hölzel et al.[12] found increases in the concentration of grey matter within the left hippocampus of healthy participants following an MBSR course. Further analyses also identified increases in the posterior cingulate cortex, the temporoparietal junction and the cerebellum, suggesting that MBSR training is associated with changes in grey matter concentration in regions of the brain that are involved in learning and memory processes, regulation of emotion, how we relate information to ourselves and perspective-taking.

Clinical trials and research into mindfulness

Formal clinical trials have been carried out and many articles and literature papers written about the effectiveness of mindfulness on a range of medical conditions and mood irregularities. The following is a small selection of such trials and research, and many more in-depth reviews, proposals and investigations can be easily found on the Internet.

Anger

- Structural equation modelling was used to investigate whether or not mindfulness could decrease anger, hostility and aggression by reducing rumination.[13] In a pair of studies, a pattern of correlations was consistent with how rumination can partially mediate a causal link between mindfulness and hostility, anger and verbal aggression. The pattern was not found to be consistent with rumination mediating an association between mindfulness and physical aggression. These findings support the idea that mindfulness could reduce rumination, which in turn could lower aggression levels.

- A mindfulness-based self-control strategy[14] was developed for an adult with a mild learning disability whose aggression had prevented him from having a successful community placement. He was taught to shift his attention and awareness from the anger-inducing situation to the soles of his feet. In time, he was able to control his aggressive behaviours better, had 6 months of aggression-free behaviour in the inpatient facility and went on to live in the community with no aggressive behaviour seen during the 1-year follow-up.

Anxiety

- Kabat-Zinn was involved in studies to determine the effectiveness of a group stress-reduction programme based on mindfulness.[15] A total of 22 participants who met the criteria for generalized anxiety disorder or panic disorder underwent a meditation-based stress-reduction and relaxation programme. Results showed significant reductions in anxiety and depression psy-chometric scores for 20 participants after treatment, as well as a reduction in the number of subjects ex-periencing panic symptoms. Follow-up at 3 years for 18 participants showed maintenance of the gains on all repeated scores, demonstrating that a time-limited group stress-reduction intervention based on mindful-ness meditation can have long-term beneficial effects on anxiety disorders.[16]

- The effectiveness of MBCT for treating insomnia symp-toms in people with anxiety disorder was investigated in an 8-week clinical trial.[17] The 19 participants showed a significant improvement in various sleep quality and anxiety/depression measures, indicating that MBCT can relieve symptoms of insomnia by reducing sleep disturbances associated with worrying.

- An MBSR programme was delivered to 14 people with social anxiety disorder, with neuroimaging per-formed before and after the course.[18] After MBSR, results showed reduced activation of the amygdala, a region of the brain that plays a role in emotional regu-lation and the fear response.

Depression

- The MBCT protocol was followed in a study to train recovered recurrently depressed people to disengage from their negative thinking patterns that might mediate relapse/recurrence.[19] Individuals were randomized to continue with treatment as usual or to also receive MBCT. Relapse/recurrence of major depression assessed over 60 weeks showed that in individuals with three or more previous episodes of depression (77 per cent of subjects), MBCT significantly reduced the risk of relapse/recurrence. For participants with only two previous episodes, MBCT did not reduce relapse or recurrence.

- In a further study using MBCT to investigate the associations between the home practice of formal or informal mindfulness and outcome, the recurrence rate of major depression in 99 participants over 12 months was reduced by about half for those who reported formal home practice at least three times per week compared with those who practised less.[20]

Anxiety and depression

- A study exploring the effect of MBCT on people with bipolar disorder or with unipolar depression was carried out, focusing on between-episode symptoms of anxiety and depression.[21] The results suggest that MBCT led to improved immediate outcomes of anxiety in the bipolar group, and reductions in residual depressive symptoms were seen in both bipolar and unipolar participants when compared with controls.
- A 2016 study examined the effect of MBCT on depression and anxiety in 80 pregnant women.[22] Results showed a significant reduction in both anxiety and

depression scores in the treated group compared with a control group who received only routine prenatal care services.

- The effects of an 8-week mindfulness stress-reduction intervention on perceived stress and psychological well-being were investigated in 70 women and one man with a previous diagnosis of cancer.[23] Those who participated in the programme had significantly increased scores on the Five Facet Mindfulness Questionnaire (see pages 91–2) compared with controls, significantly decreased perceived stress and post-traumatic avoidance symptoms, and increased positive states of mind.

Other/general

- A study was performed to investigate whether or not non-judgement of inner experience, a component of mindfulness, can influence smoking cessation.[24] Tobacco smokers (85 participants) in a randomized control trial compared mindfulness training with Freedom from Smoking (FFS), a standard cognitive-behaviourally orientated treatment. Both groups were scored on the non-judgement subscale of the Five Facet Mindfulness Questionnaire (see pages 91–2). Smokers who rarely judged their inner experience smoked less during follow-up after the mindfulness training (3.9 cigarettes/day) than did participants following FFS treatment (11.1 cigarettes/day).
- Thirty-seven individuals with psoriasis about to

undergo ultraviolet phototherapy (UVB) or photo-chemotherapy (PUVA) were studied.[25] Participants were randomly assigned to receive either the above therapy alone or additionally a brief audiotaped mindfulness meditation-based stress-reduction inter-vention. The results of the study showed that the addition of the mindfulness component to standard treatments increased the rate at which the psoriatic lesions cleared.

- A randomized controlled study was designed to inves-tigate changes in brain and immune function following an 8-week clinical training programme in mindfulness meditation delivered to healthy employees in a work environment.[26] Brain electrical activity was measured before and immediately after the programme, as well as in a group of control individuals who did not receive treatment. At the end of the 8-week period, subjects in both groups were vaccinated with influenza vaccine (to assess any changes in immune responses), and electrical activity was measured again at 4 months. Significant increases in left-sided anterior activation in the brain, associated with positive affect, was seen in subjects who undertook the programme compared with those who did not. A significantly increased immune response, as determined by the concentra-tion of antibodies in response to the vaccine, was also seen in people who did the programme compared with controls. These results show how mindfulness produces positive effects on the brain and immune function.

- A study investigated whether or not differences in brain structure are associated with low pain sensitivity as seen in Zen meditators (17 participants) compared with non-meditators (18 controls).[27] Structural MRI scans were carried out to assess the temperature required to induce moderate pain. Meditators were found to have significantly lower pain sensitivities, and this was associated with a thicker cortex in affective, pain-related regions of the brain.

- The effects of a 3-month meditation retreat was investigated on the activity of telomerase, a marker of cell viability that decreases with age and chronic psychological distress.[28] Thirty participants meditated for approximately 6 hours a day for 3 months, and blood samples were taken to assess telomerase levels. Results showed that telomerase activity was significantly greater in retreat participants than in controls, and increases in perceived control, mindfulness and purpose in life along with decreases in neuroticism were reported in the retreat group compared with controls.

3

How mindfulness can help control your mood swings

Mood swings often come out of the blue and can be quite frightening and confusing, as it is hard to identify what triggers them and we feel out of control. There may be an external reason for a sudden shift in mood, but mood swings are frequently a result of our internal processes, what we're thinking. The impact our thoughts have on our moods and how mindfulness can positively influence these processes is explored in more detail in Box 1, overleaf.

Awareness and acceptance – of your moods and yourself

Remember, mood swings themselves aren't abnormal – an alternative viewpoint is that certain people experience emotions more strongly than others, so more robust coping mechanisms are needed for them. Some people diagnosed with bipolar disorder report how the start of a more extreme mood can indicate that a phase of mania

Box 1 The thought–mood connection

Thoughts are not facts. They are just thoughts, but they have a huge impact on our moods. The particular feeling we get depends on the thoughts we have and on our interpretation of what's happened, not on the situation itself. Mood swings are very likely to be caused or exacerbated by thought processes.

Negative thinking can become a habit without us realizing, and negativity can overwhelm us to the extent that we become blind to everything else. Alternatively, cognitive avoidance may kick in, where we refuse to acknowledge our thoughts because they're too painful. We often develop safety behaviours to protect ourselves, such as avoiding situations likely to trigger a negative mood, and we believe that by avoiding thoughts, emotions or situations, this puts us in control. The reverse is true, however: the more we consciously avoid anything negative, the more likely it is to come back to haunt us, usually at highly inconvenient times.

Mindfulness teaches us to step back from our thoughts and emotions and just observe them, without allowing ourselves to be defined by them. For example, some people may interpret being turned down for a job as 'I'm a failure.' Mindfulness encourages a decentring process in which thoughts and feelings are just momentary experiences; there's no need to dwell on them or attach meaning to them. The mindful way of dealing with this situation would therefore be just to observe your emotions and thoughts about being passed over for the job . . . and let them go.

or depression is imminent. This increased awareness of their warning signs acts in a positive way, allowing them to take whatever action is needed to minimize the impact of what may follow.

It's human nature to want to turn away from anything unpleasant that causes us distress, but such experiential avoidance is not effective in the long term, and in fact it generally makes us worse. Suffering and pain cannot be avoided and are inevitable (see pages 30–2). Accepting that a range of good, bad and indifferent emotions are normal experiences helps us to accept reality. We automatically tend to judge ourselves negatively when we have mood swings – instead, try to be open-minded and switch your focus to a non-judgemental approach in line with a key principle of mindfulness. Every mood we experience is transient: it has a beginning, a middle and an end. Change in every aspect of our lives, including our sense of self (who we are), is inevitable at some point, and changing moods are just part of that natural process. If we want to change anything in our lives, including mood swings, we first need to be aware of what is going on now. Mindfulness encourages metacognitive awareness, our capacity to intuitively know what is happening and how we think. Such awareness is essential if we are to intentionally change what we are processing, how we process it or the view we take of it.

It's worth asking yourself why you feel that particular emotion at that time: is your mood valid? If you've just had some bad news, of course it's normal to feel upset. Are you currently experiencing any major life changes, such as the break-up of a relationship, the death of a loved one, moving house or starting a new job? Most people will struggle at such times, and it's OK to acknowledge that you are too. Just understanding why you have certain moods can often be sufficient to calm the mood – accept without judgement that you feel how you feel at the moment, and switch to mindfulness practice. Mindfulness quite naturally lends itself to working with mood swings as it teaches us to accept whatever is happening at that time, including changes in what we are experiencing, which are prevalent with mood swings. When we practise mindfulness regularly, we create a sense of peace and acceptance inside us, helping us to become less reactive to situations that may have been instrumental in making us feeling angry, low or anxious. Increased awareness offers us a choice about how we respond.

It can sometimes help to assign labels to thoughts and emotions that arise during practice. For example, label a noise you notice outside in the street as a 'noisy distraction' or label feeling sad when you think about your ex-partner as a 'sad emotion'. This can make it easier to let it go and switch your focus back, rather than becoming caught up in the emotions and dwelling on the negatives. Over time, notice what these labels are and identify any patterns or specific ones that crop up a lot to continue developing your awareness. The principle is to just label them and then move on – remember that these are just thoughts and emotions, they are not facts. The labels can be anything you want them to be that describes well what's going on for you, and can be as in-depth or basic as you like. Table 1 gives some examples of thoughts or feelings that may arise during mindfulness and suggests labels you may want to assign to them – feel free to change these or add to them; you may like to make your own chart on a piece of paper or in a notebook.

It's impossible to get everything right and to achieve perfection all the time, and expecting to do so is unrealistic. Perfection means reaching 100 per cent and it rarely exists – how many times have you scored 100 per cent in an exam? Probably never. A score of 70 per cent is not perfection, but it's likely to be good enough to earn you an A grade. We put so much effort into trying to achieve something that's almost impossible, it's no wonder we end up feeling stressed, frustrated and fed up

Table 1 Examples of labels for thoughts and emotions

The thought or emotion that crops up	Possible label(s) you may want to give
'I'm scared of doing that presentation tomorrow'	Fear, anticipation
'My arm itches'	Physical sensation, urge
'When I was 6, a dog bit me'	Unpleasant memory
'I'm useless at mindfulness'	Judgement, impatience
'I wanted to hit my boss today, she's an idiot'	Anger, violent thought
'I need to get milk later'	Planning thought

when we 'fail'. Suffering is caused by our desires and dis-
likes, by our dissatisfaction with what we have. At what
point is it better to acknowledge that something is 'good
enough' rather than 'perfect', and stop aiming for more,
bigger, better, higher? Is 70 per cent good enough, and
how does that translate into your situation? Humans are
not perfect creatures and never will be. As Kabat-Zinn
has stated:

> as long as you are breathing, there is more right with you than
> wrong with you.[1]

Awareness of triggers for mood swings

The more intense your mood swings are, the less likely
it is that mindfulness alone will control them sufficiently.
Awareness and understanding of your physical reactions,
thoughts and behaviours when your mood swings kick
in can help you recognize your warning signs. The trick
is to identify when you first start experiencing a change
in your mood and take action at that stage, before it
escalates. Below are non-exhaustive lists of typical body
sensations, thoughts and behaviours that are commonly
associated with anger, anxiety and low mood – which of
these triggers sound familiar to you?

Anger

A theme of injustice is frequently behind feelings of
anger. Rumination kicks in, you recall when you've felt

unfairly treated before and this fuels your anger.

As with other emotions, anger is on a continuum from mild frustration all the way to blind rage, the point at which we have lost control. It's vital to take a moment away from the situation when you feel the anger building up, before it starts charging towards the rage stage and becomes overwhelming – mindfulness will not work when your feelings are this intense. With mood swings involving anger, it's your responsibility to ensure that you keep yourself and others around you safe.

Body awareness – physical sensations you may get when angry

- Heart beating faster.
- Fists clenching, muscles tensing.
- Teeth grinding.
- Face feeling hot.
- Sweating.
- A jittery sensation or dizziness.

Cognitive awareness – thoughts you may get when angry

- 'It's not fair.'
- 'This should not be happening to me.'
- 'Things never go my way.'
- 'Here we go again; she gets all the good projects and I get the rubbish.'
- 'If one more car cuts me up today I'll go mad.'

Behaviours associated with feeling angry

- Raised voice, shouting.
- Pacing up and down, appearing agitated to others.
- Slamming things down on surfaces, throwing things about or slamming doors.
- Body stance – arms folded or invading someone's personal space.
- Being sarcastic.

Anxiety

Anxiety is built on fear – fear of something that has not necessarily happened yet, fear of becoming more emotional, fear of not being able to handle something and fear of not being in control. When we learn through mindfulness that we can handle the present, we become less fearful of the future, which means that our anxiety levels drop.

Body awareness – physical sensations you might get when anxious

- Heart beating fast, pulsating sensation in the chest.
- Breathing more quickly than normal or hyperventilating.
- Feeling shaky and dizzy more quickly.
- Nervous stomach and nausea, needing to go to the toilet.
- Sweating.
- Feeling thirsty.

Cognitive awareness – thoughts you may get when anxious

- 'What if . . .?'
- 'It's going to be terrible.'
- 'I can't do/handle it.'
- 'Others will judge me.'
- 'I'll be rejected and I'm going to end up alone.'

Behaviours associated with feeling anxious

- Seeking reassurance from others, being clingy.
- Having less patience than usual.
- Struggling to relax.
- Having a sense of dread.
- Avoiding situations or people.
- Self-harming in some way.
- Biting fingernails.
- Constantly reassuring yourself.

Low mood

Persistent rumination is strongly linked to low mood and depression – mindfulness encourages living in the present moment where the past is gone and previous negative events are over.

Body awareness – physical sensations you might get when in a low mood

- Dull ache in the stomach.
- Shoulders feeling heavy.

- All-over lethargy or exhaustion.
- Headache.
- Sense of inertia.

Cognitive awareness – thoughts you may get when in a low mood

- 'Things are never going to get better, I'm a failure.'
- 'Nobody likes me, I'm alone.'
- 'All I do is let others down.'
- 'Everyone else is doing fine; I'm the only one who isn't.'
- 'I'm never going to have a good relationship.'
- 'I keep thinking about ending it all.'

Behaviours associated with low mood

- Crying more than normal.
- Forgetfulness and poor concentration.
- Self-harming behaviours.
- Sleep difficulties – too much or not enough.
- Struggling to get up in the morning.
- Distancing yourself from others, but feeling lonely at the same time.
- Being uninterested in others and in things you used to enjoy.

Bipolar-specific triggers for highs and lows

In addition to some of the above triggers, people who have a diagnosis of bipolar disorder may recognize some of the warning signs listed below for their highs and lows.

- Difficulties with sitting still for more than a few seconds, sense of urgency.
- Believing sounds in the background are direct personalized messages.
- Thoughts of grandiosity – you're too special for something as basic as this to work.
- Not wanting to close your eyes, concerns that something might get you if you did.
- Blaming yourself for not having practised more before things got bad.
- Thoughts of being beyond help so what's the point?
- Believing no one cares about you and others would be better off if you weren't around.

You'll be able to notice some of the sensations and thoughts and recognize some of the above behaviours. All these physical sensations can be focused on intently during practice, and notice how the sensations subside. Just observe your thoughts without attaching any meaning to them and let them go, returning to focus on your body.

Use your behaviours as signals to take a few moments out, recognize they are your triggers and take action at this point to ground yourself. Regularly practising mindfulness will reduce the frequency and severity of your triggers.

Maintaining attention during mindfulness practice

If I were to ask you not to think of a goldfish smiling at you, what thought or image would immediately come into your mind? Chances are it would be a picture of a goldfish smiling, or some thought associated with it. Trying not to think of something on purpose can be incredibly challenging, but that is one of the goals of a mindful state.

Most people are continually multitasking to try to juggle work, family, home and social lives, and are bombarded by a constant stream of thoughts. The focus or anchor that we usually come back to during mindfulness practice is something within us, such as the breath, a body sensation or an emotion.

External factors such as noises and smells can distract us momentarily, as can random thoughts, and our concentration falters for a while. In mindfulness, we don't dwell on such lapses in concentration – instead, we just allow all these thoughts and other background distractions to come and go without feeling irritated, without consciously trying to push them away or judging. This involves taking a moment, acknowledging whatever distracted you, just permitting it to occupy your mind for a moment before letting it fade away naturally, and bringing your attention back to your body or emotion. A word of caution with body sensations: it may be hard using certain sensations as a focus if you have an injury or have suffered some kind of trauma in that part of the body, and it's fine to change the focus should you need to.

Approaching distractions with an attitude of openness helps us to be curious about what is happening right now. There's no need to try and hold on to thoughts during mindfulness as all thoughts and moods are temporary – remember, while you're practising, that it's not a fight! Each time you bring your attention back from random thoughts to your breath or any part of your body, you are training your brain to be more mindful, and the process is working. Your mind will wander countless times – and that's OK. As you progress with mindfulness practice, you can try changing the anchor from an internal frame of reference to something external (see page 75).

Life with more stable emotions

It's the unpredictability of mood swings that many people find difficult, especially when your mood changes very quickly. For example, perimenopausal women can feel absolutely fine one moment, then the next there's a mood akin to rage followed quickly by a deep sadness. You have no control and it feels exhausting!

The non-judgemental aspect of mindfulness encourages us to just notice negative thoughts and moods – not to focus on and then attach catastrophic meaning to them, which in turn enhances the emotional response. Previously, you may have recalled something you failed at during the day, looked on it as a failed task, expanded it in your head as 'I'm a failure' and felt very low as a consequence. Now, after practising mindfulness, a thought of something you failed at today comes into your head, you label it as 'one task that went wrong', and you just notice it and let it go. No meaning of 'I'm a failure' is attached, and no low mood arises. You're not avoiding anything; all you're doing is observing a thought and not attaching a negative interpretation to it. How much better would that be?

Mindfulness offers a robust coping mechanism that the more you practise it, the more effective it becomes – and in time it becomes less of a coping mechanism and more of a way to live your life. You'll overreact less in between practice sessions, and the calming effects you notice with each session will last longer, enabling your general mood to be more balanced and predictable. You can be in control of how intense your mood swings are and how much you let them affect you. Mindfulness cannot, however, work wonders by completely eliminating fluctuations in mood – in any case, this not desirable because it does not reflect the normal ups and downs of life.

Current mindfulness therapies

Different mindfulness therapies came about from the MBSR course devised by Kabat-Zinn, which has been widely adapted and expanded over the years. Below is a brief summary of the diverse array of programmes that incorporate mindfulness, some of which have been widely validated by clinical research.

Mindfulness-based stress reduction

As mentioned in Chapter 2, Jon Kabat-Zinn developed MBSR at the University of Massachusetts Medical Centre for treating stress and chronic pain. The format is a structured 8-week group programme of weekly sessions and daily homework with a 1-day retreat towards the end of the course, and mindfulness meditation, body scanning and straightforward yoga postures are taught. Over the years, the use of MBSR has extensively broadened, and there is now significant evidence that it can be used to improve the well-being of people with a wide range of physical and psychological conditions.

Mindfulness-based cognitive therapy

MBCT is also a structured 8-week group programme. Adapted from MBSR by Williams, Teasdale and Segal in the 1990s, it was specifically designed to treat vulnerability to a relapse of depression and combines mindfulness with certain elements of CBT for depression. Suicidal thinking can result from recurrent depressive episodes, and such thoughts may resurface whenever a low mood is re-experienced. A key feature of MBCT is to directly and intentionally focus on what is being avoided, and the programme teaches metacognitive awareness, which enables participants to view their thoughts as just thoughts and not as facts, and to break out of the repeated cycle of thoughts, behaviours and emotions. In this way, MBCT aims to reduce the distress caused by recurrent negative thoughts and prevent a reactivation of suicidal thoughts. In 2004, MBCT became one of the psychological therapies recommended by NICE in the UK for treating recurrent depression.[2]

Acceptance and commitment therapy

Acceptance and commitment therapy (ACT) came about in the early 1980s and has evolved into a variety of protocols based on relational frame therapy. It uses acceptance and mindfulness strategies and encourages people to watch themselves and see events as separate, without judgement. The goals of ACT are to embrace what is happening with our thoughts, emotions and body sensations at any moment, particularly negative ones, and to work on achieving more appropriate and desirable behaviours. There is evidence to show that ACT is effective for treating both anxiety and depression.

Dialectic behaviour therapy

Originally developed in the late 1980s to treat borderline personality disorder, DBT is a form of CBT that is also used in suicidal ideation and repeated self-harming, and therefore can be used in people with very low moods. It looks at two aspects that initially seem contradictory: accepting who you are, and working out how you can make appropriate changes to your life. This is achieved via four behavioural skills modules, one of which is mindfulness.

Mode deactivation therapy

Based on CBT, mode deactivation therapy (MDT) combines elements of mindfulness with ACT and DBT. It was originally designed to treat adolescents with mood disorders and other issues related to trauma, aggression, sexual offending and substance abuse, and aims to modify dysfunctional emotions and cognitions and undesirable behaviours. MDT works to increase awareness and acceptance using the validation–clarification–redirection (VCR) process to investigate and adjust the client's core beliefs. The mindfulness component is used for normalization purposes.

Mindfulness-based relapse prevention

Similar to MBCT, mindfulness-based relapse prevention (MBRP) aims to prevent relapses in people treated for substance abuse, and involves mindfulness training to help cope with the desire to use.[3] Attendees learn to be aware of triggers and their destructive cyclical behaviours, and are encouraged to 'ride' the waves of each urge, accepting these urges and learning that they will pass.

Mindfulness-based childbirth and parenting

Adapted from MBSR by Nancy Bardacke in the late 1990s, this 9-week childbirth education programme integrates mindfulness practices such as breath awareness and yoga with childbirth and parenting education, and can help with the stress of this journey for women and their partners.[4]

Mindfulness-based eating awareness training

Developed by Jean Kristeller in the 1980s to work with compulsive eating, mindfulness-based eating awareness training (MB-EAT) explores how we relate to our food, encourages understanding of our relationship with our bodies, and involves self-reflection, mindful meditation and eating exercises, among other components.[5]

Mindfulness-based elder care

Devised by Lucia McBee, mindfulness-based elder care (MBEC) adapts mindfulness-based interventions for the elderly and their carers, focusing more on quality of life and on what people can do rather than on their limitations.[6] It teaches skills that encourage continued growth, empowerment and stress reduction.

4

Practical mindfulness exercises for mood swings

This chapter contains guidance for mindfulness practice: it's intended to be used as guidance only, rather than as a strict set of instructions that should be followed. Take some time to read it first, get familiar with what you need to do and then begin.

Before you start

Start with an open frame of mind, and don't feel discouraged if there's no immediate 'cure' for how you're feeling as it takes time and effort. Don't worry about how many times your attention wanders – that's to be expected and provides more opportunities to train your brain to refocus. An idea of how you want your life to be different is important – why are you doing this; what changes do you want? To manage your mood swings better is a great goal in itself, but exactly what do you want to happen? Keeping a journal devoted to your experiences of mindfulness can be invaluable, allowing you to look back over the previous weeks, months and years. The book *Sheldon Mindfulness: Keeping a Journal* by Philip Cowell (see Further reading) explains the benefits of mindful journaling and how to approach the process so you get the most out of it. Maybe write some goals down in your journal and keep referring back to them, as this can help to clarify what you want to achieve. It's worth thinking seriously about it, then approach mindfulness practice with an air of curiosity and see what happens!

Setting the scene

You don't need a formal 'therapy room' for mindfulness: some quiet space anywhere you're not likely to be disturbed will do. When you become more familiar with how mindfulness works, you can use all sorts of places, such as the garden, the far end of a car park, a park bench or even in the toilets at work! Put your phone on silent, switch the TV and radio off, make sure pets are out of the room and wear clothes that aren't too tight. Maybe have a glass of water ready for afterwards, as focusing on your breath may make your throat dry.

Closing your eyes may help you connect with the emotional intensity. View strong emotions as waves. The power of even the strongest wave is not sustainable: a surge builds, the wave rises to a crescendo and then breaks and fades away. Similarly, the most intense emotion doesn't last for ever, and you can learn to ride it out by viewing the waves as emotional periods that will pass. When you have successfully surfed another wave, congratulate yourself and know that you can handle the next one, as more waves will inevitably surface. As Kabat-Zinn has said:

You can't stop the waves, but you can learn to surf.[1]

Setting a time limit when you're starting out is useful – 10, 15 minutes or whatever you feel comfortable with. The traditional posture for meditation with your legs crossed sitting upright with your back straight is ideal because it helps with breath control, but if this isn't comfortable, just sit as upright as possible. Arrange cushions and blankets around you if it helps, and make your practice time important from the start.

Selecting a focus/anchor

Having a specific focus or anchor to tune back into makes it easier to centre yourself after your mind has wandered. The focus is usually something internal, such as your breathing, physiological reactions to your emotions or other body sensations. There can be a tendency to feel less overwhelmed if you use body sensations to focus on, as emotions tend to carry more heat. Many of the exercises in this chapter suggest what your anchor should be, so follow these when you're starting out. As you become more experienced, you can decide which anchor to choose, and some experimentation may be involved. Choose one that's easily discernible when you're upset, so you don't unduly struggle to reconnect with it.

Reflections afterwards

After each practice session, take a moment to reflect on what you experienced. This is good practice even when you've been doing it for a while, as there's the potential for learning something new each time. Consider the questions listed below.

- What did you see or hear? Was there anything that you sensed?
- Did you learn anything?
- Were you more aware of any particular body sensations, thoughts or feelings?
- Did you notice a pattern? If so, what is the significance?
- If your mind wandered to the same thought, feeling or sensation more than once, were there any differences the second (or third, fourth, and so on) time – any change in intensity?
- Did you experience any fantasies?
- Was there anything positive that came up or did you feel indifferent to anything?

By reflecting on your experience after each session, it will become more obvious what triggers your mood changes. Knowing your triggers allows you to recognize when your moods may start to change, which in turn tells you to focus on particular thoughts, emotions or body sensations as soon as you can to reduce the impact of the impending mood swings. You might find that jotting a few points down in your journal after each session is useful, as it's easy to forget in between.

Incidents from the past that were particularly unpleasant at the time can occasionally resurface during practice. If this happens, don't let it freak you out – instead, be curious about the situation and view it as an opportunity for increased awareness and personal growth. During times of stress, we often recall previous negative experiences, and this may happen if you have a strong emotional response. Think back: did you deal with it sufficiently at the time of the experience, or was there a high level of avoidance on your part? Consider that this issue may need to be addressed separately before you can lay it to rest and move on. In addition, there are a couple of important points, including safety aspects, to take into consideration before you start to practise mindfulness (see Box 2, overleaf).

Box 2 A warning

1 Do not do any of these exercises while driving or doing anything where a lapse in concentration could be dangerous to yourself or others.
2 If you have any medical conditions, make sure you have your medication close by (if you have asthma, keep your inhaler within reach, for example).
3 Choose a time to start your first few mindfulness practices when you're relatively calm. Don't start if you're intensely emotional or have recently experienced something upsetting, as you may feel overwhelmed and will probably struggle. Instead, talk to someone and use whatever existing self-soothing mechanisms you have. When you feel calmer, then turn to mindfulness.

Mindful breathing

This exercise is a great introduction to practising mindfulness. It is fairly straightforward to remember and can be done whenever you have a few spare moments. The aim is to adopt a calm and non-judgemental awareness of how you are breathing, letting any thoughts and emotions just come and go without dwelling on them. Read the steps given below a couple of times first so you're familiar with what to do.

• Find somewhere comfortable and quiet, sit up as straight as possible and close your eyes.

- Shift your attention to your breathing.
- Notice how your chest rises every time you breathe in, and falls again as you breathe out.
- Focus on that rhythmical movement for a moment.
- Notice any thoughts that come into your head – that's OK, it doesn't matter what they're about, just be aware and let them pass without dwelling on them. Label them if it helps (see pages 50–1). Don't judge whether they should be there or not, just let them go.
- Bring your focus back to your breathing – to your chest slowly rising and then falling.
- Any sounds you hear inside or outside the room – just notice them, be aware and let them pass. Bring your attention back to your breathing.
- Should you feel the need to swallow, do so.
- If you notice any emotions or physical sensations, just accept that they're present without judging – again, notice them and let them go.
- Whenever you're aware that the focus of your attention has wandered away from your breathing, just recognize this has happened and calmly bring it back to your breathing, to your chest slowly rising and falling.
- After a few moments, open your eyes and gently bring your awareness back to where you are.

Your pulse rate and blood pressure may both have gone down, so take a moment to orientate yourself fully – slowly move your arms and legs a little before standing up. Repeat this exercise several times each day, make it part of your daily routine and remember to reflect on your experience as above.

The 3-minute breathing space

Originally designed by Segal, Williams and Teasdale and featured in the MBCT programme, the 3-minute breathing space[2] is a short meditation you can use as part of your regular practice or whenever you need to ground yourself. Three steps are involved, each lasting about 1 minute.

1 From a comfortable seated position, broadly notice what's happening around you. Tune in to your thoughts, feelings and body sensations for a moment, just accepting them all without trying to change them.
2 Narrow your attention down to focus on just your breath, breathing in and out, and don't try to change it. If your mind becomes distracted, be aware of where you've wandered to and refocus on your breath.
3 Extend your attention to your whole body, and notice any sensations anywhere, including inside you. Again, just let them be as they are. Gently move about for a moment before carrying on with your day.

Many videos of the 3-minute breathing space are readily available to download from the Internet (see Useful resources, page 114).

Diaphragmatic breathing

This technique is often taught in complementary therapies as it has a powerful relaxation quality and can help with stomach cramps in irritable bowel syndrome. It pushes the diaphragm (the muscle separating the chest and abdominal cavities) downwards to increase the amount of oxygen that gets into the lungs.

Put one hand on the centre of your chest and the other on your stomach, and breathe in and out normally a few times. Chances are that the hand on your chest is moving while the one on your stomach is pretty much still. Try changing that: with each inhalation consciously push your stomach out while trying to keep your chest from moving. As you exhale, bring your stomach back in, keeping your chest still and repeat, slowly. This technique can be tricky to get the hang of, but is worth persevering with as it teaches you to concentrate intently on your body.

Mindful eating

The well-known mindfulness exercise of eating a raisin features in the MBSR course devised by Kabat-Zinn and can be adapted to eating anything mindfully.[3] It's quite simple in principle: eat something and really notice what the experience is like. The point of mindful eating is to teach you how to start noticing things to a degree you probably won't have done before. It demonstrates beautifully how mindfulness can be a normal everyday event, and helps us understand practically what is meant by awareness and focus, and the depths to which we can go to achieve this. Mindful eating is an exercise you can do anywhere, including at your desk if you're not taking a separate lunch break away from work.

- Take your time and look at your food before starting – notice the different colours, shapes and textures.
- As you put each piece of food in your mouth, let it rest a few seconds on your tongue before starting to move it around or chew. Be aware of what the food feels like in your mouth, on your tongue and as you move it about.
- Notice the sound of yourself eating, how the different smells and tastes merge and change as you chew.
- Be aware of the texture of each mouthful, slowly savouring and chewing thoroughly.
- Notice any thoughts or emotions that crop up.
- What does it feel like to swallow the food?
- Wait to reload your fork or spoon until you have completely finished each mouthful.
- Remain seated for a moment, notice your breathing and reflect on your experience.

It's amazing what a difference eating mindfully can make to how much you enjoy your meals, and eating this way can also help to reduce compulsive eating behaviours. As Kabat-Zinn has stated:

When we taste with attention, even the simplest foods provide a universe of sensory experience, awakening us to them.[4]

Simple noticing practices

These are for practising using an external anchor instead of an internal one. You can focus on any everyday object wherever you are (being, as always, aware of safety issues), and you can be as creative as you like. The focus need only be for a short while. Each time you pick an object to work with, really study it in as much depth as you can. Notice its colours, shape, symmetries, asymmetries, textures, smells, if it's moving and so on. Afterwards, reflect on how that was and what you noticed that surprised you. Some examples of external objects to practise with include:

- a flower, leaf or tree
- a spiders' web in the garden, with rain on it
- rings or other jewellery, or an easily visible tattoo
- any item at a checkout when you're in a long queue
- the bubbles in a glass of fizzy wine
- a marking on the floor of the bus or train
- your shoe
- a pen or pencil on your desk
- the taps when you're in the bath
- even the handle of the bathroom door when you're on the loo!

There really is the opportunity to do mindfulness every-where, as Kabat-Zinn has said:

> If mindfulness is deeply important to you, then every moment is an opportunity to practice.[1]

Specific mindfulness exercises for mood swings

By this point, you have first-hand understanding of what mindfulness is, know what set-up suits you best and can redirect your focus to the breathing. Now you're familiar with using a straightforward anchor to keep your mind focused, try shifting your attention to the thoughts that give rise to your emotions and mood swings.

Exercise in awareness

Practise the following exercise[3] for viewing any thoughts, emotions or body sensations that come up as distant objects. The principle here is to view what is happening from a slightly removed or detached position – you're observing rather than totally experiencing by shifting from focusing to awareness. This reduces the likelihood of feeling overwhelmed.

- Start by focusing inwards on your breath – breathe in and out, slowly and deeply. Do this for a few moments.
- Move your mind outwards and observe any thoughts, emotions or body sensations as objects floating down a stream – just notice them coming closer, watch them

float by and see them disappear into the distance. No need to judge or analyse, just observe.

- Next, pick any object out of the stream and focus on it, just letting other thoughts, emotions or sensations drift by. Notice and focus on anything new that comes from this object.
- After a moment, place the object on a leaf and watch it float away.
- Reflect on what you experienced.

This helps you learn to face highly charged thoughts and emotions.

Exercise in working with specific moods

Next, look at the emotions that trouble you: anger, anxiety and/or low mood. The principle is to consciously bring up thoughts that lead to your mood swings so you can work with a specific emotion. You will also see how differently your body feels as the emotions fade. Practise this when you are in a calm frame of mind, so when your mood swings are charging towards intense, your body and mind will have learnt how they need to respond.

- Imagine a situation or bring up thoughts you know are triggers for your anger, anxiety or low mood.
- Concentrate on those thoughts, feel the emotions and label whatever comes up.

- Focus on that emotion and be deliberate about what this moment actually is right now rather than what you think it should be.
- Keep focusing, bringing your attention back to the emotions when your mind wanders.
- Maintain your attention on the emotion for as long as you can.
- If it's overwhelming, view the emotion as an object floating down the stream (as above) and just observe it floating by.
- Staying with the emotion, notice how your body sensations and thoughts diminish.
- Reflect on how this experience was for you.

You can also use this sequence to manage mood swings when they spontaneously occur. When you start to ruminate about the past or worry about the future, both of which we know initiate and maintain mood swings, consciously switch your attention to your body sensations, notice what your emotions are and focus. When a mood swing is extreme, however, it can be hard to focus on that emotion or an associated thought. Many people find it's best to just focus on the body sensation and wait for that to subside: focus as intently as you can, and if you feel overwhelmed, view whatever is happening as an object floating by you downstream, to distance yourself and keep yourself safe. Once this wave has subsided, reflect on what just happened.

Guidance for mindfulness with mood swings

This section explores how you can adapt mindfulness to specific aspects of your anger, anxiety and low mood experiences. The focus can be any behaviour or thought associated with the mood, or the mood itself. Creating mindfulness scripts for the potential range of body sensations, thoughts and behaviours associated with mood swings would be very repetitive: in any case, no single script will work for everyone as we all experience our moods in individual ways. The principle is the same, however, regardless of whether you're focusing on a behaviour, thought or emotion: notice what's come up for you, label it and refocus. You may just want to sit and focus on your fists clenching when you feel angry, for example, and that's fine. Alternatively, a recurring thought may cause you to feel very low, so just focus on that emotion or any body sensation that is associated with it.

There are some common thoughts, physical sensations and behaviours that are associated with mood swings (see pages 52–7), and for each of anger, anxiety and low mood, there is some suggested guidance to follow below. You do not need to work through each step in turn as some points may not apply to you: read each section first to get an idea of what to look out for. There may be additional things that come up for you – that's fine, just go with them. If you have worked through the above mindfulness practices, you will be proficient enough to adapt the following guidance to your specific situation and needs.

The guidance can be followed when you are experiencing a mood swing, if you have the opportunity for some privacy, but can also act as a practice session. In the latter case, as you may have done with the exercise in managing specific moods, think of a scenario that will guarantee you feel angry, anxious or low, and begin. The more practice you get at sitting with strong emotions, the easier it will become. Should you need to use an external anchor throughout any of the exercises, then do so.

Mindfulness in anger

Focus for this practice: the behaviour of raising your voice, commonly experienced with anger.

- Notice where you feel this – in your throat or head; does your mouth feel dry?
- Do you feel like you want to invade someone's personal space and yell in their face?
- Notice whether or not you are pushing your neck forwards; are your shoulders forwards and up; are your hands twitching?
- What else is happening in your body – are you breathing more quickly; do your face and neck feel warm?
- What thoughts are you having – any fantasies of

violence, passive aggression or wishing harm on someone or something?

- Are any thoughts of injustice from the past coming up? How is the situation similar; are the people involved the same?
- What stops you from handling this in a calm and non-confrontational manner?

Just notice whatever comes up and focus on each aspect. Wait a few moments and reflect on your experience.

Mindfulness in anxiety

Focus for this practice: dizziness, which is a common symptom of anxiety.

- Notice exactly where you feel this – on the top of your head or elsewhere?
- What's happening to your posture; what are your shoulders doing; are you moving about more than normal?
- Is your vision normal or blurred?
- How is your breathing?
- What else is happening in your body – is anything shaking?
- What thoughts are you having – are you totally in the here and now or is your mind racing off to possible future scenarios that all have a negative theme? Is anything coming up from your past?

- Are you having any catastrophic thoughts?
- What stops you from being able to handle these thoughts without this level of anxiety?

Just notice whatever comes up and focus on each aspect. Wait a few moments and reflect on your experience.

Mindfulness in low moods

Focus for this practice: I'm a failure, which is a common belief behind a low mood.

- Notice where you feel it in your body – stomach, muscles, heart, somewhere else?
- How heavy does your body feel?
- Describe your current energy level.
- Notice what your body language looks like.
- In what way are you a failure – in everything or is one scenario more prominent?
- Are there other more accurate explanations of what's happened? Were you let down; was the situation out of your control, for example? What haven't you considered?
- What other thoughts are coming up? Are you recalling other occasions when you've thought you're a failure – what happened at that time and how does it relate to what's happening now?
- What stops you from realizing that you're a success in many ways?

Just notice whatever comes up and focus on each aspect. Wait a few moments and reflect on your experience.

A word about bipolar disorder

Mindfulness cannot cure bipolar disorder, but some people find it can help to stabilize their moods better when used alongside prescription medication. Stress is known to be a key trigger for both the manic and depressive phases, so reducing stress levels using mindfulness can make the highs and lows more manageable in the longer term.

Mindful awareness while moving

Mindfulness can involve physical activity as well as just sitting down! Wherever it's safe to do so, you can use the same principles of intently focusing, noticing and letting distractions come and go without judging. Perform all movements slowly and deliberately, be aware what your body is doing at that moment, and notice how this awareness guides you away from your usual ruminative thought patterns and worries. When your focus wanders, just notice, label and refocus.

Below are a few examples of how you can be mindful while moving. All can be used when you're calm or experiencing a mood swing, depending on what suits you and what's appropriate. Remember to reflect on how it was for you afterwards.

Walking

This is effective when you're in any mood. It can be done around your home, in the garden or somewhere quiet. Focus on the ground a few steps in front of you, relax your shoulders as much as possible, and notice the sensation of your feet on the ground before you start to move. Take a slow step forward, notice how your foot feels as it leaves the ground, makes contact with the floor, rolls forward, how your balance changes as the other foot lifts, and so on. Notice changes in your posture as you move, how the different muscles tense and relax, notice your rhythmic pace and how your arms naturally swing. Keep walking at an easy pace for a few moments.

Jogging

This can be particularly useful if you have excess energy to burn off or are feeling angry and need to remove yourself from a situation for a while. Make use of how repetitive and monotonous the jogging action can be to help you notice the rhythm of your legs and arms, observe how your breathing changes, notice your feet hitting the ground, be aware of which muscles you can feel working more. Are there any sensations on or in your face, such as the wind blowing, the warmth of the sun or your cheeks moving up and down? Be aware of any other parts of your body that are moving and focus on those for a moment. Does anything hurt? Feel free to increase or decrease your jogging pace as suits.

Swimming

Notice the sensation of the water over your body, float for a moment and experience the natural movement of the water; see how your body responds. Slowly start swimming, whatever stroke you want to do, bringing your attention to every part of your body in turn, noticing which muscles are working harder, being aware of any change in temperature on your arms and shoulders as they briefly come out of the water and then are submerged again, being aware of your breathing pattern and the rotation of your body in the water, focusing on the rhythm and so on. If you wish to swim faster and burn some energy up, choose one action to focus on, such as breathing, turning your head, your hands entering the water or your legs kicking.

Warning: wherever you're swimming, watch out for obstacles! If you are swimming in a pool, be careful when approaching each end that you don't whack your hands on the tiles. If you're in open water or the sea, make sure you sight regularly (for people, animals, boats, any sort of floaters), and I'd recommend only doing mindful open water swimming for a few moments at a time so you don't swim too far away from support!

Washing up!

Observe the bubbles before you put your hands in; are they moving, making any noise, glistening in the light? Notice the temperature change as you submerge your hands, how the brush or pad feels as you pick it up, how it feels to exert pressure on the items in the bowl; notice all the different sensations you can. What happens to the bubbles as you continue with your actions? Can you see bits of food floating about in the water? Notice how every movement you make is different from the last.

Other things you can mindfully do during the day include brushing your teeth, having a bath or shower, drying your hair, painting your toenails, gardening, throwing a ball at the wall or just lying in bed. You can also have a bit of fun with moving mindfulness: mindfully walk down the chocolate or cake aisle in the supermarket and notice any smells, body sensation, thoughts – is your mouth watering? Have an external focus of something at the end of the aisle, and as you walk towards it notice what happens in your body and see if any thoughts or emotions come up. As you turn down the next aisle, be aware of how your body sensations have changed; what's different? You can be as creative as you like with mindfulness!

The body scan

This is excellent for releasing tension in the body and involves focusing your attention on and intently noticing every part of your body in turn. The body can store stress pretty much anywhere and the body scan often releases it, so don't be concerned if you find this quite an emotional experience (it's normal for feelings of fear, sadness, anger and frustration to come up).

- Lie on the floor or the bed in a comfortable position, arms by your sides (and support your head if you need to).
- Close your eyes and just focus on your breathing for a few moments.
- Slowly and deliberately bring your attention to every part of your body in turn, starting with the toes or head (it doesn't matter which end you start at), making sure you do each leg and arm as well. If any part feels sore, stiff, achy, tingly, heavy or numb, tune in to that sensation and focus intently on it. If the sensation intensifies, just experience what that feels like and wait for the sensation to subside naturally.
- As with any mindfulness exercise, when your mind wanders off, just notice, accept and refocus without judgement.
- Once the sensation has subsided at that position, continue scanning the rest of your body, stopping and focusing on any part where you notice a different or unusual sensation.
- Continue until you notice no further specific sensations.
- Reflect on the experience.

Mindful visualizations

Consciously and intently focusing on anything will help to train your brain and can reduce stress levels. Most of us will go on to automatic pilot, ruminate and imagine negative scenarios at some point: try turning this around and sit quietly for a while, imagining only positive scenarios, or use simple objects to focus on what you find relaxing. Notice the difference physically, emotionally and cognitively when you think positively compared with when you are surrounded by negativity. Here are a few suggestions.

• Instead of imagining someone else getting a promotion at work and focusing on how bad that would be, visualize you being promoted or see yourself in a different, better job.
• Bring up a situation that may anger you, but instead imagine that you cope calmly with it and just let the event go without feeling annoyed.
• Breathe in the scent of your favourite flower and concentrate on its scent and nothing else.
• Imagine a balloon floating around, collecting all your negative and pessimistic thoughts and worries; just watch them all floating away into oblivion with the balloon and notice feeling differently about them.
• Visualize yourself successfully coming out of your mood swings – what would that be like; how would

it change your relationships; what would you do differently?

There are many guided meditations and visualizations readily available on the Internet, including some great ones on YouTube. You can also personalize your visualizations – use your imagination!

Measuring your mindfulness progress

Over time, your experiences during mindfulness practice will change: thoughts that used to elicit a strong response are likely to carry less of an emotional charge; they may stop coming up altogether and alternative thoughts may arise. This leads to a change in self-perspective (how you view yourself), and there is neuroimaging evidence for this phenomenon.[5] People who practise mindfulness regularly find their rumination and distress levels are generally reduced, and safety behaviours they have devised to protect themselves are no longer needed. These are such fundamental changes that having some kind of a measure to show what has been happening would seem advisable. Keeping track of how you feel is a great way to monitor your progress, maintain motivation and provide encouragement for when times are tough. It doesn't have to be time-consuming – just a few minutes at the end of each day is sufficient.

Daily mood diary

If you are prone to rapidly changing moods, keeping a check on how you are feeling over a period of several weeks can help you see how your moods are starting to even out or change. Table 2 is an example of a basic template that you could draw out in your journal to record how much practice you are doing, what moods are prominent throughout the day and how intense those moods are. It takes just a couple of minutes each day to fill this in, but at the end of a few weeks it is really useful to be able to look back and see how things are different. Chances are you have been trying to avoid strong or painful feelings in the past, but now you are facing them in mindfulness, so don't be discouraged if your moods temporarily worsen when you're starting out, as this is quite normal.

Table 2 Example of a daily mood diary

Day	Number of sessions	Total minutes of mindfulness	Moods	Rate mood intensity from 0 to 10 (0 = lowest, 10 = highest intensity)
Monday				
Tuesday				
Wednesday				
Thursday				
Friday				
Saturday				
Sunday				

Five Facet Mindfulness Questionnaire

Several different scales exist that measure various aspects of the mindfulness experience, including the Freiburg Mindfulness Inventory, the Mindful Attention Awareness Scale, the Kentucky Inventory of Mindfulness Skills, the Cognitive and Affective Mindfulness Scale, the Southampton Mindfulness Questionnaire, the Philadelphia Mindfulness Scale and the Toronto Mindfulness Scale. They may all have their individual shortcomings, however.[6] Mindfulness itself cannot be quantified as it is a very subjective experience and is not readily observable by others, which may indicate that self-reporting questionnaires are more appropriate.

Baer et al.[7] devised the Five Facet Mindfulness Questionnaire, which was collated from some of the above reporting tools and incorporates items with the strongest psychometric properties. Hölzel et al.[5] explain how it measures the following aspects of mindfulness practice in terms of:

1 **observing the experience** noticing internal and external stimuli such as body sensations, emotions, thoughts, sights, sounds and smells;
2 **describing these stimuli** labelling them, such as 'my anxiety sensations';
3 **acting with awareness** paying attention to what's happening now instead of being on autopilot or avoiding;

4 **not judging your inner experience** resisting the temptation to evaluate your body sensations, thoughts and emotions;

5 **not reacting to your inner experience** allowing thoughts and feelings to come and go naturally, without getting caught up in them.

You can download the questionnaire for free.[8] It includes 39 straightforward questions, and for each, you select which one of five possible answers applies most appropriately for you at that time, ranging from 'never or very rarely true' to 'very often or always true'. The download contains instructions on how to take the test and score it. It is worth doing this every month or two, depending on how many mindfulness sessions you do, and seeing what happens to your scores for each of the five sections. It should take about 15–20 minutes to complete.

Common difficulties experienced

I can't focus on a body sensation, my mind keeps wandering

That's OK, just step back for a moment, notice what your mind wanders to, label it, accept that you're struggling and let go of any judgement. Acknowledging a distraction helps acceptance. Remember, we have no conscious control over what pops into our minds, so judging yourself is pointless. What emotions do your thoughts bring up? It's sometimes easier to reach a body sensation via an emotion you can name. If in doubt about what to come back to, choose your breath or something you can physically feel, such as your back on the chair or the soles of your feet on the floor. With practice, the time it takes to return to your body sensation of choice should reduce, and you will be able to hold your attention for longer before your mind wanders off again.

I'm scared of how overwhelming my emotions might be

When distressing thoughts or emotions come up, it is best to fully acknowledge their presence and label them, before intentionally refocusing your attention as a deliberate action. Not acknowledging what's upsetting is termed experiential avoidance (see page 49), and it maintains emotional distress.[9] Instead, approach the feeling with an attitude of curiosity. When it eventually subsides, which it will do, your brain has learnt to cope with it. Mindfulness itself cannot create thoughts or emotions that were not originally there – the difference is, you are acknowledging them now instead of pushing them away. If you fear the emotions will become overwhelming, however, try viewing them as objects passing downstream and disappearing, and then refocus your attention (see pages 76–7).

I just don't feel emotional enough for mindfulness today

It's fine if you don't have strong emotions coming up, as it's not essential to experience intense emotional reactions every time you practise. Try focusing on whatever is happening for you, notice what it is doing, and go with whatever comes up, even if, temporarily, that's nothing.

My bum's gone to sleep and I can't focus on anything else!

Being still for a prolonged period of time can cause stiffness and pain in the muscles and joints, so move about if you wish to get into a more comfortable position. Or instead of being tempted to shift your position to relieve your stiffness, try focusing your attention directly on where you feel the discomfort and adopt a non-judgemental attitude, in particular towards any thoughts of 'I can't stand it!' Kabat-Zinn has proposed that if we are exposed to pain sensations for a lengthy period without any catastrophic consequences, we may become desensitized, leading over time to a reduction in emotions brought about by the pain.[10] So if we just acknowledge and accept the discomfort, it tends to fade – try it and see what happens; be curious. It goes without saying that if you have a pre-existing medical condition, this may not be appropriate, so consult your GP for advice.

I can't get any quiet time to myself

A very common problem! There are many possible solutions depending on your individual situation: drive to a quiet location to be alone for 10–15 minutes, try it when you're in bed, rope in other members of your family (kids included!), go around to a friend's house, sit in the garage or shed, or take a detour to somewhere quiet on the way to or from work. You could even set your alarm earlier in the morning and use this time before anyone else is up. Many people swear that by starting the day with some mindfulness, they are much calmer for the entire day. If you want to try it enough, you will find a way!

How to incorporate mindfulness into your lifestyle

Don't wait until you're at crisis point, or hang on for a significant date such as a new year's resolution, to start mindfulness practice – just start whenever you can. Scheduling a regular time (preferably daily) for yourself is important, as little and often will ensure you feel the benefits more when your mood swings are at their most intense. Over time, you will become more aware of your triggers, be able to act on them and gain relief more quickly. Change is not immediate – it takes time – and the more you practise mindfulness, the better you become at it. There will be days where it seems like it's just not happening; just accept that's how it is today and try again tomorrow. Don't let it discourage you. Have patience.

Depending on what works best for you, there are many different ways you can incorporate mindfulness into your life. There is a wide selection of courses available online, as well as YouTube features, books and audio files, for example, and there are mindfulness groups you can join or taught courses you can sign up to – search online for what's available in your local area. Group support can be invaluable as this is a great way to meet like-minded people. In addition, having regular sessions at set times adds structure to your week and gives you a valid reason to get some time away from the house! Some people find that recording a script on their phone so they can play it during practice works well for them, or there are many such scripts readily available on the Internet and free to download if you prefer. As you can see from the range of exercises and activities in this chapter, mindfulness can be applied to pretty much anything. Take time each day to notice and appreciate things around you, whatever you're doing and wherever you are.

Note: when you become more adept at mindfulness, you will undoubtedly have grown as a person and be responding differently to situations and towards others, including your loved ones. Relationships may change, which can be unsettling for you and for those close to you. On the one hand, your loved ones will be pleased that your mood swings have quietened down and you are feeling more content in yourself, but on the other hand the change may be a little unsettling for them. Be aware of this possibility and be patient with them while they too adjust.

5

Additional tips for managing mood swings

It's likely that aspects of your lifestyle are playing a role in your mood swings, so it's worth looking at what you're doing throughout the course of each day to identify where you can make adjustments that may help.

Food and drink

What you consume

Eating the right kinds of food means that your body gets the fuel it needs to function properly. A diet containing a high proportion of processed and fried foods is known to cause mood swings, as well as lead to anxiety and low moods. Balancing healthy, unprocessed foods with the occasional little bit of what you fancy is considered reasonable advice. The following are suggestions for how altering aspects of your diet could have a beneficial effect on your mood swings.

Foods

Low-glycaemic index (GI) foods are relatively slowly broken down by the body and raise blood glucose levels steadily, in contrast with high-GI foods, which the body digests quickly and which raise blood sugar levels rapidly, causing a surge of energy followed by a crash. Such a rapid variation in glucose levels is known to play havoc with emotional regulation. By all means eat some high-GI foods (such as white bread and biscuits), but just have small amounts every now and then instead of a lot every day. Lower GI foods to go for include porridge, whole-wheat pasta, hummus, lentils, peanuts and non-starchy vegetables.

Several studies have shown that unstable blood sugar levels can be linked with quite violent mood swings, and the increased risk of developing diabetes is well documented. One study investigated the link between blood glucose levels and self-reported mood in 34 adults with insulin-dependent diabetes mellitus.[1] The patients completed a mood/symptom checklist (featuring items describing physical symptoms and positive or negative mood states) just before measuring their glucose levels. Results showed that low blood glucose tended to be associated with negative moods, particularly nervousness. Positive mood items on the checklist were almost always associated with high glucose levels, but high levels were also often correlated with negative mood states that tended to be more about anger and sadness than nervousness.

Proteins contain amino acids such as tryptophan, which is needed to make the naturally occurring mood stabilizer serotonin. The body cannot make tryptophan on its own so we need to include it in our diet (from, for example, meat, eggs, tofu, salmon, cheese and some nuts). There is evidence to suggest that when carbohydrates and proteins are eaten together, the body, via a complex mechanism, increases the uptake of tryptophan into the brain to stimulate serotonin production.

Folate (vitamin B9) is needed for the synthesis of neurotransmitters (such as serotonin), and folate deficiency has been linked to low mood. We need a regular intake of folic acid from foods such as broccoli, lentils, spinach and some beans, as the body cannot store it.

Chillies contain capsaicin, which induces the release of endorphins, the body's natural painkillers, providing a 'feel-good' effect. Curcumin, the active agent in turmeric, which is added to many curries, has recently been proposed for the potential treatment of depression. In a 2014 trial involving 60 patients diagnosed with major depressive disorder, the effects of the antidepressant fluoxetine (the active agent in Prozac), curcumin and a combination of fluoxetine and curcumin were investigated.[2] Results were assessed after 6 weeks using the Hamilton Depression Rating Scale, and the mean changes in score were shown to be comparable across all three groups. Curcumin was also found to be well tolerated by all the patients. This provides evidence that curcumin may be an effective and safe treatment for major depressive disorder.

Probiotic yogurt containing 'good' gut bacteria, such as *Lactobacillus* and *Bifidobacterium*, can boost your immune system, making you less susceptible to colds and other infections that affect your moods. Prebiotic supplements provide specific food for these bacteria, enhancing their activity.

It is a good idea to vary your diet in general and include plenty of brightly coloured fruit and vegetables to ensure that your body gets a good range of vitamins and minerals. Consider eating raw vegetables too, as cooking can destroy some vitamins.

Caffeine

One of the effects caffeine has on the body is to stimulate the production of adrenaline, a key neurotransmitter involved in the fight–flight–freeze response (see pages 8–9). Excessive caffeine will cause your body to react as if a threat has been perceived, and you will be likely to feel nervous, shaky and on edge. It is also common to develop urinary tract irritation from regularly having too much caffeine, leaving you prone to bladder infections that can affect your mood. If you currently have large amounts of caffeinated drinks, don't stop them suddenly, as you will be likely to develop caffeine withdrawal symptoms and experience a banging headache in the short term. Try alternating caffeinated and decaffeinated drinks for a while and slowly reduce your caffeine intake over time.

Several studies undertaken on animals have shown that caffeine consumed in smaller amounts may, however, act as a mild antidepressant by stimulating the release of certain neurotransmitters. One group of researchers investigated the association between coffee and caffeine consumption and suicide risk within three large-scale cohorts totalling over 200,000 men and women.[3] Caffeine consumption was assessed and deaths from suicide during the study period were recorded. By comparing the number of cups of caffeinated coffee drunk, those who consumed modest amounts (2–4 cups per day) were found to have been at about half the risk of suicide as those who drank less or no caffeinated coffee. In contrast, results of a different study showed that the risk of suicide in people who drank at least eight cups of coffee a day was 58 per cent higher than in people who drank moderate amounts.[4] It would appear that consuming modest amounts of caffeine is reasonable advice.

Alcohol

Many people think that alcohol is a stimulant because a few drinks can lift our mood and make us feel more lively and sociable, but it's actually a depressant in the effects it has on the body. Indeed, one of the effects seen with regular and excessive drinking is that serotonin levels are reduced, making us more susceptible to low moods. Excessive drinking causes us to become disinhibited and often leads to angry outbursts, which can have unfortunate and sometimes legal consequences. Any kind of mood swings are common in people who drink too much, so watching your alcohol consumption is important – particularly during times when you know you are going to be more stressed.

Recreational and other drugs

The side effects of some prescription medications, for example, progesterone-only contraceptive pills, and corticosteroid tablets taken for more severe asthma, may include mood fluctuations, so check the information leaflet provided with the medication or ask your pharmacist. If mood alterations are listed as potential side effects or you think your mood swings may be connected to your prescription drugs, do not suddenly stop taking the medication without seeking advice from your GP.

Most recreational drugs have an effect on neurotransmitter levels so will affect your mood in one way or another. The website Talk to Frank provides straightforward and accurate information about different kinds of recreational drugs and explains the short- and long-term effects of taking them, including how they commonly cause mood swings. It also has a wonderful section showing videos of the effects different drugs have on the brain (see page 114).

When you consume it

The timing of when you eat can be as important as what you eat. Irregular meals or long gaps in between them causes erratic insulin and blood sugar levels and, as mentioned above, fluctuating glucose levels are known to cause significant and unpredictable mood changes. Eat soon after getting up in the morning even if you don't feel like it, as your body needs fuel to kick-start itself and stop you feeling sluggish. A full-blown cooked breakfast isn't necessary if you can't stomach large amounts of food first thing: fruit and yogurt, toast, a couple of boiled eggs or a quick bowl of cereal are infinitely better than nothing. Don't skip lunch even if you're really busy, as you'll experience a mid-afternoon slump in energy, and try not to eat a huge meal late in the evening as your body won't have time to digest it properly. Avoid caffeine within a few hours of going to bed as it may keep you awake, so try switching to decaffeinated drinks in the evenings. Also watch out for caffeine lurking in the ingredients labels of some fizzy drinks.

Note crash diets are inadvisable – they don't work in the long term, play havoc with insulin levels and your moods, and can cause deficiencies of minerals and vitamins. In addition to being aware of what you are eating and when, keep well hydrated – even mild dehydration can easily cause moodiness and lethargy. Sip water throughout the day to ward this off – and drink extra when exercising.

Sleeping habits and daily schedules

It is well known that lack of proper sleep leads to irritability and lethargy, and ensuring you get adequate amounts of sleep is essential if you are susceptible to mood swings. Make your bedroom as conducive to sleep as possible, and avoid using phones or watching TV late at night (see page 22). Keeping a relatively consistent schedule throughout the week may help, so try to avoid very late nights followed by extra-long lie-ins at weekends, as taking a few days to get back into your normal routine is likely to worsen your mood swings.

The circadian rhythm is a combination of physiological, mental and behavioural changes in the body that, among other things, regulate our sleep–wake cycle. It balances body temperature and the release of hormones: melatonin, for example, is produced in the evening to promote sleep. As well as being associated with difficulties in mood regulation, abnormal circadian rhythms have been linked to insomnia, fatigue, depression, bipolar disorder and seasonal affective disorder.

Light is an important factor in controlling the circadian rhythm, so reducing the amount of light in the bedroom with blackout blinds during summer months can help. In winter, try to expose yourself to as much natural light as possible. Night workers may be more prone to mood swings, as when their body is telling them that it's the natural time to sleep, they are in fact trying to be at their most alert. Particularly at risk are workers whose shifts vary throughout the week.

Social life versus you time

Getting the right balance between family life, work and social activities where we communicate with others and having time alone for ourselves can be difficult. Scheduling time each day to provide a mindfulness focus just for you is advisable, as it will become a routine for the rest of your family as well as for you. Depending on what you prefer, set some time aside first thing in the morning and/or in the evening – up to an hour or whatever suits you best. Sometimes we can have too much time to ourselves, in which case consider taking up a new hobby or finding local social groups to join.

Exercise

The benefits of regular physical exercise are well documented: you don't have to start training for a marathon tomorrow, as just light or moderate levels of exercise will give you health benefits, make you feel better in general and improve your sleep. Before starting any new form of exercise, it is wise to consult your GP and get a quick health check to make sure everything is OK. Do anything from gentle to intense exercise, whatever works for you. You can take up walking, jogging, swimming, cycling, exercise classes at your local gym or even trampolining if you like! Training for an event (such as a 5K run) can help keep you focused and give you a goal to work towards, so you can measure your progress. Consider using activities such as yoga and tai chi in particular as moving mindfulness sessions, making the most of the deliberate movements involved to help increase body awareness.

Technology

Mobile phones

If you are glued to your phone all day and feel naked without it, maybe it's time to think about putting it to one side for a few hours towards the end of the day. Blue light emitted by phone screens can keep you awake (see page 22), so keep phone use to a minimum before bedtime. Try reading or using this time of day for mindfulness practice instead and, if you wake in the night, avoid playing on your phone!

Social media – not always a good idea?

Many of us take to social media such as Facebook and Twitter to see what's happening with friends or celebrities, organize social events, kill some time or have a rant. This may not be the ideal place to seek support when you are feeling particularly stressed or down, however, as you could absorb any negative emotional tones of whatever you are reading.

Researchers investigated whether the mood of Facebook

posts was contagious or not by looking at more than a billion updates from approximately a million users over a three-year period (without having access to any names or personal information).[5] They studied posts from people who were Facebook friends with someone in a rainy location, but who were not themselves in a place where it was raining. Results showed that for every negative post made by the friend in the rainy area, the person in a non-rainy place wrote 1.29 more negative posts compared with normal, implying that negative posts tend to have a knock-on negative effect on others' emotions.

Interestingly, they found that positive posts were likely to cause others to write happier posts too, indicating there really is a strong possibility we absorb the moods of our friends or connections on social media sites. Until we start reading the latest Facebook posts or scrolling through recent tweets, though, how do we know whether it is likely to improve or worsen our mood? We don't. So maybe it's worth considering steering clear of Facebook, Twitter and other social media while your mood swings are particularly bad, otherwise you may inadvertently worsen your mood. There are, however, many groups and organizations you can access via Facebook, Twitter and LinkedIn, for example, relating to mindfulness that do offer great support and advice – so concentrate on these instead when you need help the most and skip the usual gossip.

Television

What you watch on TV can have a significant impact on your mood. The news, for example, is intensely negative, and many crime programmes, soaps, documentaries and charity stories can leave you feeling drained. These are all best avoided if you are feeling low – choose less intense and lighter programmes instead. Nature documentaries can have a very relaxing influence too, if you fast-forward through the parts where some unfortunate creature gets disembowelled!

Apps

Many mindfulness, relaxation and self-soothing apps are readily available, many of them free or provided at a very low cost. What you prefer is a highly individual choice, so recommending a specific app is outside the scope of this book. Make use of the free introduction offered by some apps, and check online reviews first for whatever you download to ensure it is what you're looking for. There are some considerations around mindfulness apps that might affect your choice.[6]

General tips

Making some relatively small changes to our lives can give us a lift and reduce stress levels. When we implement and maintain several of these changes, we are more likely to notice a difference in how frequently and intensely we experience our mood swings. Here are some suggestions for things you can try.

- Track your mood swings in a journal – this helps to monitor your progress and it is often easier to identify patterns if information is written down.
- Keep active and consider trying new forms of exercise – yoga and tai chi, in particular, complement mindfulness well.
- Be aware of boundaries – do you need to push back in your relationships with others; is it appropriate for you to say 'No' to their demands at times? Also be aware of whether you may be overstepping the mark with some people – do you need to pull back at all?
- Do you self-sabotage? If so, consider why you do this, what you hope to gain from it and what purpose it actually serves. Use mindfulness to explore this.
- Look after personal hygiene properly – take care of your body.
- Listen to music to give your mood a lift, but don't listen to the same songs repeatedly and certainly make sure you don't wallow in sad songs when you are in a low mood!
- If you know a difficult period or challenging situation is ahead (the anniversary of a loved one's death is coming up or you are starting a new job, for example), plan ahead to reduce your stress, maintain contact with

friends and family and make sure you don't skip your regular mindfulness sessions.

A combination of being aware of the above, watching what you eat and drink and regularly practising mindfulness can have a very powerful and positive effect on your mood swings.

Supporting those with mood swings

Living or working with those who experience regular mood swings can be very challenging. At times it may seem like the entire world revolves around them, and people can end up tiptoeing around in their presence. A key factor is understanding their mood swings: by all means help them by discussing when you feel things are starting to get out of control, but it is important to let the responsibility for managing their mood swings lie with them and not with you. At home, you can help provide structure and have an input into a healthier lifestyle, but remember that you too are allowed an opinion, and they do need to acknowledge how they are affecting you. It is sometimes harder at work, where it is less appropriate and often inadvisable to be frank with a colleague or boss! If you have already tried a calm and constructive conversation with them and that hasn't worked, consider asking for 'off the record' advice from your HR department or another boss. If you are struggling with your colleague's behaviour at work, it's likely that others are too.

I hope this book has given you a good understanding of what mood swings are all about, what causes them and how you can use mindfulness to help manage them. The more you progress with your mindfulness practice, the more you'll feel able to control your mood swings, and you will find they will become less intense over time. Keep practising and enjoy!

Useful addresses

Anxiety UK
Zion Community Centre
339 Stretford Road
Hulme
Manchester, M15 4ZY
Tel.: 08444 775 774
Website: www.anxietyuk.org.uk

Bipolar UK
11 Belgrave Road
London SW1V 1RB
Tel.: 0333 323 3880
Website: www.bipolaruk.org

CALM (Campaign Against Living Miserably)
PO Box 68766
London SE1P 4JZ
Tel.: 0800 585858
Website: www.thecalmzone.net

Cruse Bereavement Care
PO Box 800
Richmond
Surrey, TW9 1RG
Tel.: 0808 808 1677
Website: www.cruse.org.uk

Mind
15–19 Broadway
Stratford
London E15 4BQ
Tel.: 0300 123 3393
Website: www.mind.org.uk

Mood Swings
36 New Mount Street
Manchester, M4 4DE
Tel.: 0161 832 3736
Website: www.moodswings.org.uk

PAPYRUS (Prevention of Young Suicide)
Lineva House
28–32 Milner Street
Warrington
Cheshire, WA5 1AD
Tel.: 0800 068 4141
Website: www.papyrus-uk.org

Rethink Mental Illness
89 Albert Embankment
London SE1 7TP
Tel.: 0300 5000 927
Website: www.rethink.org

Samaritans
Freepost RSRB-KKBY-CYJK
PO Box 9090
Stirling, FK8 2SA
Tel.: 116 123 (UK and ROI, 24 hours)
Website: www.samaritans.org

Sane Line
St Mark's Studios
14 Chillingworth Road
Islington
London N7 8QJ
Tel: 0300 304 7000
Website: www.sane.org.uk

Talk to Frank
Tel.: 0300 123 6600
Website: www.talktofrank.com

Useful resources

British Association for Counselling and Psychotherapy (BACP)
www.itsgoodtotalk.org.uk/therapists
Directory to help with finding local counsellors.

CBT Register
www.cbtregisteruk.com/Default.aspx
Directory to help with finding a local cognitive behavioural therapist accredited by the British Association for Behavioural and Cognitive Psychotherapies (BABCP) or the Association for Rational Emotive Behaviour Therapy (AREBT).

Counselling Directory
www.counselling-directory.org.uk
Directory to help with finding a local counsellor or psychotherapist.

Flight–flight–freeze response
www.psychologytoday.com/blog/evolution-the-self/201507/trauma-and-the-freeze-response-good-bad-or-both
Excellent explanation of this response to difficult situations.

Free Mindfulness Project
www.freemindfulness.org/download
Free guided exercises.

Guided mindfulness meditation practices
www.mindfulnesscds.com
Guided mindfulness meditations from Jon Kabat-Zinn.

Headspace
www.headspace.com
Meditation app.

Mind
www.mind.org.uk/information-support/guides-to-support-and-services/seeking-help-for-a-mental-health-problem/private-sector-care/#.WB5Ij8s5fFI
Guide to finding a private counsellor.

Mindfulnet.org
www.mindfulnet.org
For information on mindfulness and research. See also the page at: <www.mindfulnet.org/page6.htm> for suggestions for mindfulness books, websites and apps.

Moodswing
www.moodswing-app.com
Social networking app.

NHS
www.nhs.uk/Service-Search
Directory to help with finding a GP and other services.

NHS's Moodzone
www.nhs.uk/Conditions/stress-anxiety-depression/Pages/low-mood-stress-anxiety.aspx
Helpful information on stress, anxiety and depression and a mood self-assessment questionnaire.

Oxford Mindfulness Centre
www.oxfordmindfulness.org
For information on mindfulness and research. See also the page at: <www.oxfordmindfulness.org/learn/resources> for books, videos and a mindfulness app.

Talk to Frank
www.talktofrank.com
For information on drugs, and videos of the effects drugs have on the brain.

UK Council for Psychotherapy (UKCP)
www.psychotherapy.org.uk/find-a-therapist
Directory to help with finding a local therapist.

YouTube
www.youtube.com/watch?v=CVW_IE1nsKE
Example of the 3-minute breathing space by Professor Mark Williams.

Notes

Introduction

1 Scheerhout, John (2016) 'Stressed-out GMP officers are being trained in "mindfulness" to help them counter anxiety and depression', *Manchester Evening News*, 16 June. Available online at: <www.manchestereveningnews.co.uk/news/greater-manchester-news/stressed-out-gmp-officers-being-11479491>.

2 Booth, Robert (2014) 'Politicians joined by Ruby Wax as parliament pauses for meditation', *The Guardian*, 7 May. Available online at: <www.theguardian.com/society/2014/may/07/politicians-ruby-wax-parliament-mindfulness-meditation>.

3 Walker, Rob (2016) 'Close your eyes and breathe: schools sign up to mindfulness', *The Guardian*, 23 October. Available online at: <www.theguardian.com/education/2016/oct/23/mindfulness-school-lessons-pupil-stress>.

1 About mood swings

1 Mind (2013) 'Mental health facts and statistics: How many people have mental health problems?', Mind's website at: <www.mind.org.uk/information-support/types-of-mental-health-problems/statistics-and-facts-about-mental-health/how-common-are-mental-health-problems>.

2 Mental Health Foundation (2013) 'Starting today: The future of mental health services', Final Inquiry report, September', Mental Health Foundation. Available online at: <www.mentalhealth.org.uk/sites/default/files/starting-today.pdf>.

3 Altena, E., Micoulaud-Franchi, J. A., Geoffroy, P. A., Sanz-Arigita, E., Bioulac, S. and Philip, P. (2016) 'The bidirectional relation

between emotional reactivity and sleep: From disruption to recovery', *Behavioral Neuroscience*, 130(3): 336–50.

4   NHS Choices (2016) 'Bipolar disorder', NHS Choices' website at: <www.nhs.uk/Conditions/Bipolar-disorder/Pages/Introduction. aspx>.

5   British Broadcasting Corporation (2006) 'The secret life of manic depression: Everything you need to know about bipolar disorder'. Available online at: <downloads.bbc.co.uk/headroom/bipolar/bipolar.pdf>.

6   Rethink Mental Illness (n.d.) 'Borderline personality disorder (BPD)', Rethink Mental Illness's website at: <www.rethink.org/diagnosis-treatment/conditions/borderline-personality-disorder -bpd>.

7   American Psychiatric Association (2013) *Diagnostic and Statistical Manual of Mental Disorders* (5th edn). Washington, DC: American Psychiatric Publishing.

8   Chetty, S., Friedman, A. R., Taravosh-Lahn, K., Kirby, E. D., Mirescu, C., Guo, F. et al. (2014) 'Stress and glucocorticoids promote oligodendrogenesis in the adult hippocampus', *Molecular Psychiatry*, 19(12): 1275–83.

9   Mitchell, Ed (2013) 'It is time to stop treating mental health as a "cinderella" issue', Blog, 24 October, NHS England's website, at: <www.england.nhs.uk/2013/10/ed-mitchell-3>.

10 Care Quality Commission (2015) 'Right here right now: People's experiences of help, care and support during a mental health crisis', Care Quality Commission, June. Available online at: <www.cqc.org.uk/sites/default/files/20150611_righthere_mhcrisiscare_summary_3.pdf>.

11 Manber, R., Schnyer, R. N., Lyell, D., Chambers, A. S., Caughey, A. B., Druzin, M. et al. (2010) 'Acupuncture for depression during pregnancy: A randomized controlled trial', *Obstetrics and Gynecology*, 115(3): 511–20.

12 Barbini, B., Benedetti, F., Colombo, C., Dotoli, D., Bernasconi, A., Cigala-Fulgosi, M. et al. (2005) 'Dark therapy for mania: A pilot study', *Bipolar Disorders*, 7(1): 98–101.

2 *About mindfulness*

1 National Institute for Health and Care Excellence (2017) 'Finding guidance', NICE. Available online at: <www.nice.org. uk/guidance>.

2 Kabat-Zinn, J. (1994) *Wherever You Go, There You Are: Mindfulness meditation in everyday life*. New York: Hyperion.

3 Teasdale, J. D. and Chaskalson, M. (Kulananda) (2011) 'How does mindfulness transform suffering? II: The transformation of dukkha', *Contemporary Buddhism*, 12(1): 103–24.

4 IMD UK (2012) 'Is it habit yet?', post 2 August, IMD's website at: <imduk.org/tag/hebbs-law>.

5 Bishop, S. R., Lau, M., Shapiro, S., Carlson, L. E., Anderson, N. D., Carmody, J. et al. (2004) 'Mindfulness: A proposed operational definition', *Clinical Psychology: Science and Practice*, 11: 230–41.

6 Shapiro, S. L., Carlson, L. E.; Astin, J. A. and Freedman, B. (2006) 'Mechanisms of mindfulness', *Journal of Clinical Psychology*, 62(3): 373–86.

7 Brown, K. W., Ryan, R. M. and Creswell, J. D. (2007) 'Mindfulness: Theoretical foundations and evidence for its salutary effects', *Psychological Inquiry*, 18(4): 211–37.

8 Baer, R. A. (2003) 'Mindfulness training as a clinical intervention: A conceptual and empirical review', *Clinical Psychology: Science and Practice*, 10: 125–43.

9 Hölzel, B. K., Lazar, S. W., Gard, T., Schuman-Olivier, Z., Vago, D. R. and Ott, U. (2011) 'How does mindfulness meditation work? Proposing mechanisms of action from a conceptual and neural perspective', *Perspectives on Psychological Science*, 6: 537–59.

10 Hölzel, B. K., Ott, U., Hempel, H., Hackl, A., Wolf, K., Stark, R. et al. (2007) 'Differential engagement of anterior cingulate and adjacent medial frontal cortex in adept meditators and non-meditators', *Neuroscience Letters*, 421(1): 16–21.

11 Farb, N. A., Segal, Z. V., Mayberg, H., Bean, J., McKeon, D., Fatima, Z. et al. (2007) 'Attending to the present: Mindfulness meditation reveals distinct neural modes of self-reference', *Social Cognitive and Affective Neuroscience*, 2(4): 313–22.

12 Hölzel, B. K., Carmody, J., Vangel, M., Congleton, C., Yerramsetti, S. M., Gard, T. et al. (2011) 'Mindfulness practice leads to increases in regional brain gray matter density', *Psychiatry Research*, 191(1): 36–43.

13 Borders, A., Earleywine, M. and Jajodia, A. (2010) 'Could mindfulness decrease anger, hostility, and aggression by decreasing rumination?', *Aggressive Behavior*, 36(1): 28–44.

14 Singh, N. N., Wahler, R. G., Adkins, A. D. and Myers, R. E. (2003) 'Soles of the feet: A mindfulness-based self-control intervention for aggression by an individual with mild mental retardation and mental illness', *Research in Developmental Disabilities*, 24(3): 158–69.

15 Kabat-Zinn, J., Massion, A. O., Kristeller, J., Peterson, L. G., Fletcher, K. E., Pbert, L. et al. (1992) 'Effectiveness of a meditation-based stress reduction program in the treatment of anxiety disorders', *American Journal of Psychiatry*, 149(7): 936–43.

16 Miller, J. J., Fletcher, K. and Kabat-Zinn, J. (1995) 'Three-year follow-up and clinical implications of a mindfulness meditation-based stress reduction intervention in the treatment of anxiety disorders', *General Hospital Psychiatry*, 17(3): 192–200.

17 Yook, K., Lee, S. H., Ryu, M., Kim, K. H., Choi, T. K., Suh, S. Y. et al. (2008) 'Usefulness of mindfulness-based cognitive therapy for treating insomnia in patients with anxiety disorders: A pilot study', *Journal of Nervous and Mental Disease*, 196(6): 501–3.

18 Goldin, P. R. and Gross, J. J. (2010) 'Effects of mindfulness-based stress reduction (MBSR) on emotion regulation in social anxiety disorder', *Emotion*, 10(1): 83–91.

19 Teasdale, J. D., Segal, Z. V., Williams, J. M., Ridgeway, V. A., Soulsby, J. M. and Lau, M. A. (2000) 'Prevention of relapse/recurrence in major depression by mindfulness-based cognitive therapy', *Journal of Consulting and Clinical Psychology*, 68(4): 615–23.

20 Crane, C., Crane, R. S., Eames, C., Fennell, M. J., Silverton, S., Williams, J. M. et al. (2014) 'The effects of amount of home meditation practice in mindfulness-based cognitive therapy on hazard of relapse to depression in the Staying Well after Depression Trial', *Behaviour Research and Therapy*, 63: 17–24.

21 Williams, J. M. G., Alatiq, Y., Crane, C., Barnhofer, T., Fennell, M. J. V., Duggan, D. S. et al. (2008) 'Mindfulness-based cognitive therapy (MBCT) in bipolar disorder: Preliminary evaluation of immediate effects on between-episode functioning', *Journal of Affective Disorders*, 107(1–3): 275–9.

22 Yazdanimehr, R., Omidi, A., Sadat, Z. and Akbari, H. (2016) 'The effect of mindfulness-integrated cognitive behavior therapy on depression and anxiety among pregnant women: A randomized clinical trial', *Journal of Caring Sciences*, 5(3): 195–204.

23 Bränström, R., Kvillemo, P., Brandberg, Y. and Moskowitz, J. T. (2010) 'Self-report mindfulness as a mediator of psychological well-being in a stress reduction intervention for cancer patients – a randomized study', *Annals of Behavioral Medicine*, 39(2): 151–61.

24 Schuman-Olivier, Z. D., Hoeppner, B. B., Evins, A. E. and Brewer, J. (2014) 'Finding the right match: Mindfulness training may potentiate the therapeutic effect of non-judgment of inner experience on smoking cessation', *Substance Use and Misuse*, 49(5): 586–94.

25 Kabat-Zinn, J., Wheeler, E., Light, T., Skillings, A., Scharf, M. J., Cropley, T. G. et al. (1998) 'Influence of a mindfulness meditation-based stress reduction intervention on rates of skin clearing in patients with moderate to severe psoriasis undergoing phototherapy (UVB) and photochemotherapy (PUVA)', *Psychosomatic Medicine*, 60(5): 625–32.

26 Davidson, R. J., Kabat-Zinn, J., Schumacher, J., Rosenkranz, M., Muller, D., Santorelli, S. F. et al. (2003) 'Alterations in brain and immune function produced by mindfulness meditation', *Psychosomatic Medicine*, 65(4): 564–70.

27 Grant, J. A., Courtemanche, J., Duerden, E. G., Duncan, G. H. and Rainville, P. (2010) 'Cortical thickness and pain sensitivity in zen meditators', *Emotion*, 10(1): 43–53.

28 Jacobs, T. L., Epel, E. S., Lin, J., Blackburn, E. H., Wolkowitz, O. M., Bridwell, D. A. et al. (2011) 'Intensive meditation training, immune cell telomerase activity, and psychological mediators', *Psychoneuroendocrinology*, 36(5): 664–81.

3 How mindfulness can help control your mood swings

1 Kabat-Zinn, J. (1990) *Full Catastrophe Living: Using the wisdom of your body and mind to face stress, pain and illness.* New York: Delacorte.

2 National Institute for Health and Care Excellence (2017) 'Find guidance', NICE's website at: <www.nice.org.uk/guidance>.

3 Information about Mindfulness-Based Relapse Prevention (MBRP) is available from MBRP's website at: <www.mindfulrp.com>.

4 Mindfulness-Based Childbirth and Parenting (MBCP) Program (2017) 'Mindful birthing: Training the mind, body and heart for childbirth and beyond', Mindful Birthing's website at: <www. mindfulbirthing.org>.

5 Mindful Eating (2015) 'About mindful eating and MB-EAT', Mindful Eating's website at: <www.mb-eat.com>.

6 McBee, Lucia (2008) *Mindfulness-Based Elder Care.* New York: Springer. See also Lucia McBee's website at: <www.luciamcbee. com>.

4 Practical mindfulness exercises for mood swings

1 Kabat-Zinn, J. (1994) *Wherever You Go, There You Are: Mindfulness meditation in everyday life.* New York: Hyperion.

2 Segal, Zindel (2016) 'The three-minute breathing space practice', *Mindful*, 8 June. Available online at: <www.mindful.org/ the-three-minute-breathing-space-practice>.

3 The Mindful Word (2012) 'MBSR: Mindfulness-based stress reduction exercises', 22 April, The Mindful Word's website at: <www.themindfulword.org/2012/mbsr-mindfulness-based-stress-reduction>.

4 Kabat-Zinn, J. (2005) *Coming to Our Senses: Healing ourselves and the world through mindfulness.* New York: Hyperion.

5 Hölzel, B. K., Lazar, S. W., Gard, T., Schuman-Olivier, Z., Vago, D. R. and Ott, U. (2011) 'How does mindfulness meditation work? Proposing mechanisms of action from a conceptual and neural perspective', *Perspectives on Psychological Science*, 6(6): 537–59.

6   Baer, R. A. (2011) 'Measuring mindfulness', *Contemporary Buddhism: An Interdisciplinary Journal*, 12(1): 241–61.

7   Baer, R. A., Smith, G. T., Hopkins, J., Krietemeyer, J. and Toney, L. (2006) 'Using self-report assessment methods to explore facets of mindfulness', *Assessment*, 13(1): 27–45.

8   Baer, Ruth (2014) 'Five Facet Mindfulness Questionnaire (FFMQ)', Ruth Baer's website at: <www.ruthbaer.com/academics/FFMQ.pdf>.

9   Teasdale, J. D. and Chaskalson, M. (Kulananda) (2011) 'How does mindfulness transform suffering? II: The transformation of dukkha', *Contemporary Buddhism*, 12(1): 103–24.

10   Kabat-Zinn, J. (1982) 'An outpatient program in behavioral medicine for chronic pain patients based on the practice of mindfulness meditation: Theoretical considerations and preliminary results', *General Hospital Psychiatry*, 4(1): 33–47.

5 Additional tips for managing mood swings

1   Gonder-Frederick, L. A., Cox, D. J., Bobbitt, S. A., Pennebaker, J. W. (1989) 'Mood changes associated with blood glucose fluctuations in insulin-dependent diabetes mellitus', *Health Psychology*, 8(1): 45–59.

2   Sanmukhani, J., Satodia, V., Trivedi, J., Patel, T., Tiwari, D., Panchal, B. et al. (2014) 'Efficacy and safety of curcumin in major depressive disorder: A randomized controlled trial', *Phytotherapy Research*, 28(4): 579–85.

3   Lucas, M., O'Reilly, E. J., Pan, A., Mirzaei, F., Willett, W. C., Okereke, O. I. et al. (2014) 'Coffee, caffeine, and risk of completed suicide: Results from three prospective cohorts of American adults', *World Journal of Biological Psychiatry*, 15(5): 377–86.

4   Tanskanen, A., Tuomilehto, J., Viinamäki, H., Vartiainen, E., Lehtonen, J. and Puska, P. (2000) 'Heavy coffee drinking and the risk of suicide', *European Journal of Epidemiology*, 16(9): 789–91.

5   Coviello, L., Sohn, Y., Kramer, A. D. I., Marlow, C., Franceschetti, M., Christakis, N. A. et al. (2014) 'Detecting emotional contagion in massive social networks', *PLoS ONE*, 12 March, 9(3):

DOI: 10.1371/journal.pone.0090315. Available online at: <http://journals.plos.org/plosone/article?id=10.1371/journal.pone.0090315>

6 Tlalka, Stephany (2016) 'The trouble with mindfulness apps', *Mindful*, 10 August. Available online at: <www.mindful.org/trouble-mindfulness-apps>.

Further reading

Alidina, S. (2010) *Mindfulness for Dummies*. Chichester: John Wiley.

Cowell, P. (2016) *Sheldon Mindfulness: Keeping a Journal*. London: Sheldon Press.

Hazeley, J. A. and Morris, J. P. (2015) *The Ladybird Book of Mindfulness*. Loughborough: Ladybird Books.

Segal, Z. V., Williams, J. M. G. and Teasdale, J. D. (2013) *Mindfulness-Based Cognitive Therapy for Depression* (2nd edn). New York: Guilford Press.

Stahl, B. and Goldstein, E. (2010) *A Mindfulness-Based Stress Reduction Workbook*. Oakland, CA: New Harbinger.

Teasdale, J., Williams, M. and Segal Z. (2014) *The Mindful Way Workbook: An 8-week program to free yourself from depression and emotional distress*. New York: Guilford Press.

Wax, R. (2013) *Sane New World: Taming the mind*. London: Hodder & Stoughton.

Wax, R. (2016) *A Mindfulness Guide for the Frazzled*. London: Penguin.

Williams, M., Teasdale, J., Segal, Z. and Kabat-Zinn, J. (2007) *The Mindful Way Through Depression: Freeing yourself from chronic unhappiness*. New York: Guilford Press.

About the author

Caroline Mitchell is an accredited counsellor, an Eye Movement Desensitization and Reprocessing (EMDR) practitioner and a trauma therapist, as well as having worked in private practice and in homicide bereavement. She is also a freelance writer and proofreader and has worked in medical publishing for over 20 years, but *Mood Swings* is her first book. In her spare time, she loves the outdoors and has recently discovered an unexpected passion for open-water swimming and triathlons. She lives in Greater Manchester, on the edge of the West Pennine Moors.